BULLS
&
BEARS

Life lessons from the financial markets

How to be the Chief Executive of your own life

Bulls & Bears   *Life lessons from the financial markets*

Publisher:

MindPower Publications
www.mindpowerpublications.com

Layout, Drawings & Cover Design: Elof Gribwagen

Copyright © 2013
by Siphiwe Moyo
www.siphiwemoyo.co.za

ISBN-13: 978-1494432348
ISBN-10: 149443234X

This book is copyright under the Berne convention. No part of this book may be reproduced in any form, or by any means, without prior permission in writing from the author and publisher.

ALL RIGHTS RESERVED

Bulls & Bears *Life lessons from the financial markets*

Bulls & Bears   Life lessons from the financial markets

 ## CONTENTS

Acknowlegements..9

Introduction..11

Bulls and Bears: The lessons before the lessons......14

In life you will mess up, get over it............................20

You can get back up again – A lesson
from the Rand..26

The death of the bull market is not the bad
news everyone believes it to be..................................28

The Agency Problem..36

"Success is the sum of small efforts
repeated day in and day out." R Collier....................38

Get the principles right when you are still "small."......44

"Wall street people learn nothing and
forget everything." Benjamin Graham......................49

The intelligent investor realizes that shares
become more risky as their prices rise and
less risky as their prices fall."..................................56

Human beings are like derivatives: your value depends on what happens to the value of another asset..............58

Price is what you pay, value is what you get." Warren Buffet..............63

Change your words and change your world..............65

Exceptionally high earnings growth rates are unsustainable for long periods..............73

Pricing power is derived from differentiation, not by being a commodity business..............75

"If you are born poor it is not your fault but if you die poor it is." Bill Gates..............78

If it works for someone else, it doesn't mean it will work for you..............85

Investing in yourself, just like investing in the stock market, is cheaper than you think..............90

Don't panic over price changes..............93

Experience always counts..............99

When we see a game, they see business..............104

Delayed Gratification..............106

Stop lying, you are not self-made..............111

Price Follows Earnings..............116

Finding a good mentor is like
finding a great investment adviser...........................120

All trends eventually end...122

Overconfidence is as bad as lack of confidence......128

People judge you harshly when you're
untested, it's not personal: focus on the
work and they'll come around....................................132

You cannot judge someone's potential
by their past. Give people a chance..........................135

On the other hand: A lesson from the Economists...143

There is something called too much
diversification – Those who get to the
top are focussed and single-minded..........................147

Bull markets always last longer than
Bear markets – be bullish..153

Past performance is no
guarantee for future results..157

Humiliation is a part of life, Deal with it......................163

If your friend ever asks you who
Robert Mugabe is, terminate that friendship!............167

In the financial markets, just like in life:
nobody cares how good you used to be...................171

Contrary to popular belief, the
world owes you absolutely nothing..........................174

Small now, large later...178

Be patient..182

The job of analysts is to talk – The job
of Chief Executives is to run a business...................187

Bibliography...193

ACKNOWLEDGEMENTS

Now to Him who is able to do exceedingly, abundantly, above all that we ask or think, according to the power that works in us, to Him be glory in the church by Christ Jesus to all generations, forever and ever. Amen. Thank You Lord for saving me and for giving me gifts and talents to serve my generation.

A special word of thanks belongs to the most beautiful woman in the world, my wife Thabang for all the sacrifices she made during this project. Thank you for understanding. I love you, you are my life. To my daughter Obakeng, thank you for making me smile.

To my two mothers, Ntombi Moyo and Selina Matlwa, my dad Elias Mlaba, my brother Jabulani Moyo and the rest of my family, thank you. I don't believe in this 'self-made' theory. I am here because of you, ngiyabonga.

Thanks to my spiritual parents, Bishop Mosa Sono and Pastor Gege Sono for their outstanding leadership. I would also like to thank Dr EMK Mathole for the many lessons you taught me while accompanying you in your speaking engagements. Thanks to Pastors Fani and Morwesi Gxoyiya, Nkosana and Nancy Tsoliwe, Bongani and Bernice Zwane for all you have taught me. To my speaking mentor Billy Selekane, CSP - thank you for the time you always give me.

To all my friends, colleagues, leaders and church mates, thank you for all the support.

Thanks to Granny Manamela for the great work she did editing this book.

INTRODUCTION
HOW IT ALL STARTED...

I fell in love with the general financial markets and the equity market in particular between the year 2000 and 2001. The early 2000s were a very interesting period in the South African financial markets. The South African Financial Markets were going through financial liberalisation, which is a fancy term meaning that people outside the country were starting to buy our local securities and the locals were also showing interest in foreign securities.

I was in my late teens, staying in an informal settlement in the South of Johannesburg called Orange Farm and I was studying for my first degree full-time and working at Mr Price clothing store part-time. I moved to Orange Farm in 1997 from Soweto and never really made friends for a while because most people didn't think I was "cool" enough. I found solace in two things, radio and books. I listened to business radio and read a lot of business books, which was unheard of in my neighbourhood. The more I read and listened to radio, the more aloof I became and my love for the financial markets kept growing.

My first degree had absolutely nothing to do with financial markets; I studied Human Resources followed by a BCom (Hons) and an MBA. While studying for my MBA, I was working for one of the top four banks in South Africa and my love for the financial markets was "getting out of hand". I even considered changing careers in 2008 right in the middle of the global financial crisis. I registered for a program in financial markets at the South African Institute of Financial Markets (SAIFM) but later dropped out because I realised that I don't want to make this my career.

I'm a born professional speaker and facilitator. I still qualified as a Certified International Retail Banker, interestingly from an academy that advocates separating retail banking from investment banking.
This book is not about the financial markets so if you were hoping for some tips on investing, unfortunately you have the wrong book. It is about the life lessons I have learned from the financial markets. I'm still

amazed by the incredible life lessons that can be derived from the financial markets.

To make understanding the book easier, I will only define what the bull and bear markets are. The terms bull market and bear market describe upward and downward market trends, respectively and can be used to describe either the market as a whole or specific sectors and securities.

BULL MARKET

A bull market is associated with increasing investor confidence, and increased investing in anticipation of future price increases (capital gains). A bullish trend in the stock market often begins before the general economy shows clear signs of recovery.

BEAR MARKET

A bear market is a general decline in the stock market over a period of time. It is a transition from high investor optimism to widespread investor fear and pessimism.

Enjoy the lessons and apply them because the practice of knowledge is called wisdom.

BULLS AND BEARS
THE LESSONS BEFORE THE LESSONS...

Before we get into the core lessons of this book, I think it's important to first look into the animals themselves because there's so much to learn from them and some of the market-related lessons I discuss have been influenced by the animalistic lessons.

Let's take a look at the bulls- they've come a really long way and serve multiple purposes beyond just meat and dairy. This shows the bull's flexibility because it doesn't serve a single purpose. The bull doesn't just do one thing so grab the lesson here, be a bull and learn to be flexible. Engage and participate in different things but never loose focus on your key purpose.

Back in the days, bulls were often used as a form of transport and today, this hardly happens because things have changed and the bulls are moving with the times. Likewise, you must be relevant and live in the present. Fulfil your relevant purposes and demands in all spheres of your life (work, home, relationships and other organisations).

Another thing about bulls is that they only eat certain things, they don't just chow anything. Similarly, bears also have their own type of food. In general, these animals both have a 'special bull/bear diet.' The fact here is, these animals know what to eat and don't just eat anything they come across. They know what's good for them and feed off it.

Likewise, watch what you feed off! Not just with regards to food but be careful of what you believe, listen to, and take into your mental system. Food is for your health and that's why you must also eat words that are healthy for your soul. I can see you're already doing that because you're reading this book.

Even though bears belong to the same species and animal kingdom, just like the twins, bears are all different. For example, the black bear is different from the brown and polar bear even though they're all bears. Moreover, brown bears are all brown yet different nonetheless. Bulls also share similar characteristics and belong to the same species yet aren't necessarily the same. Likewise, we are all human beings yet all different so know yourself and embrace your uniqueness. Don't try to fall into a category you don't belong to. Polar bears don't desire to be brown bears so don't loose yourself trying to be like others, just stick to you!

In dealing with bulls, whether in bull-fighting or milking, these animals aren't handled anyhow. They are handled in particular ways and with great caution. Why am I telling you all this? Because you also shouldn't handle people in any way you please. We're all different and it's very important to understand each other and be sensitive to others so we can relate well and live harmoniously. Just like the bulls, maltreatment affects behaviour and people's attitudes are influenced by how you treat them. So be careful of how you talk, relate and treat others, it always goes a long way.

Bulls have certain postures and strategies used under threat. For example, they may lower their head and shake it from side to side and their horns go up when they attack. Bears on the other hand may use clawing, biting and rubbing teeth as a form of strategy under attack. The point is, these animals know what to do and when to do it. They can surely put up a fight.

You must also know how to cope in difficulties. Know your weapons and how to utilize them because when you're in your own bear season, you must be ready for battle and know which steps to take. In addition, when bulls attack, they go head on with the threat and when a bull is attacking you, the worst mistake is to turn your back on it. Therefore, face your battles and challenges. Fight them head on and stop ignoring or running away from them. Fight and deal with it now because if you don't it will always come back to haunt you somehow. Issues buried alive never die! They simply fall into deep sleep and will always be triggered to wake up one way or the other.

Bulls that are kept with cows are usually less aggressive than those kept alone. Just like the bulls, we're better off when we have others. We are social beings, and we need each other. Life is not for the loners. Isolation and solitary confinement are not an option, so be there for others and allow others to be there for you because in this life, we need each other.

Unfortunately for us, we can never afford to be like bears in certain aspects. For example, bears eat all summer long and become dormant in winter. This is unrealistic for humans because for us it's unfortunately called laziness, which is also not an option if we are to make it in life. Furthermore, we unfortunately cannot sleep during the tough winter seasons of our lives. We just don't have the bear's privilege of sleeping 3 months or more during winter. We can never wait until conditions are suitable for us to do all that we need to.

Even though it's always advisable to adopt the strength and courage of a bear, you can clearly see that you cannot afford to adopt the above-mentioned bear behaviours. You must always be active because for humans, even though we may toil and have more than enough, it's never wise for us to just stay relaxed, comfortable and settled. We continuously have to strive, not only to survive and succeed but to stay on the survival and successful seat.

It's quite ironic how bears are associated with cuteness and with the soft pretty teddy bear some of you go to bed with. Well in reality, bears aren't all that cute, they kill. Even bulls may seem tame yet can turn and severely injure or kill a person. On a final note, bears are very alert animals. They are very vigilant and pay attention to their surroundings. It's also significant for us to be aware of what's happening with and around us. Pay attention to your environment so you don't get sidetracked and overwhelmed by unexpected events. Prior preparation always ensures great performance. So don't allow yourself to go blind when you can be watchful, lest the storm takes you by surprise.

And now we head on to the lessons learned from the Bulls and Bear Markets, enjoy…

IN LIFE YOU WILL MESS UP, GET OVER IT.

The reality about life is that nobody's perfect. No-one makes the correct assumptions and choices at all times. We all make mistakes; it's inevitable and therefore inescapable. We have seen it ourselves; the greatest people have stumbled, faltered and got it all wrong. It's just as Benjamin Graham said, "No matter how careful you are, the one risk no investor can ever eliminate is the risk of being wrong." Is this not true about life? As long as you live in this life, you will be wrong.

Although this is the case, it's ironic how disappointed people get when an honourable man, say a pastor for example does something immoral. The congregation and other people aware of his position judge and humiliate him. This shows the natural human condition of always expecting the best from people we honour and respect as though they're infallible. Moreover, it shows how we struggle to accept everyone's fallible humanity which makes it inevitable for each and every one of us to make errors and blunders.

The reality is that we all mess up so never think you're an exceptional case because no-one is an exception to this rule. It's really funny how some people think they are. I was at a conference once and when I said this, a young lady said to me "Excuse me Siphiwe, I don't mess up" and I was like, excuse me ma'am, (with the same tone and attitude) "I know your boyfriend and you've already messed up."

Anyway, you may choose to see yourself as the absolute Miss/Mr Perfect but this is life and life is lived by humans, and human beings are absolutely not infallible. Whether you're a senior or junior, experienced or inexperienced, no matter who you are, where you're from and how much you've accomplished, you are guaranteed to make the wrong choices, incorrect assumptions and even say the wrong things.

Einstein himself said it, "Anyone who has never made a mistake has never tried anything new". This is the truth about life. It comes with no manual, not even a heading or a bit of a clue. The behaviourists will tell you, we are born in a blank slate, meaning a blank mind with no knowledge whatsoever. All we do throughout life from the early developmental stages is to try new things, experiment and see what the outcome will be. This is how learning occurs.

We ought to be like little children, try new things and fail, knowing that in the end we will succeed. No-one was born walking or talking for that matter, but look at you today, you walk and talk as though it was the first thing you were born doing. Did it just automatically happen? Of course not! You fell multiple times and couldn't say a sentence without sounding Greek, but from those mistakes u learned and have now mastered the art of walking and talking so to speak.

When you look at the financial markets and the number of people who have messed up, it's a substantial lot. Take Roger Babson, one of the greatest economists to have lived. In 1928, he was an economist and forecaster and this is what he said, "The election of president Herbert Hoover is going to lead to a great prosperity in America." The following year in 1929,

America and the world went through the Great Depression. This was after a very experienced economist had predicted great prosperity and the results were America's biggest financial crisis instead.

The other organisation that messed up was the International Monetary Fund (IMF). Back in October 2008, just after the investment bank Lehman Brothers collapsed, the International Monetary Fund unveiled its forecasts for growth in 2009. The IMF is the global lender to national governments; its economic pronouncements are highly respected. So what did it predict? The US would grow 0.1% in 2009, countries in the euro zone 0.2% and the world as a whole 2.6%. The actual outturns were declines of 3.5%, 4.2% and 2.6% respectively.

The IMF messed up big time here so if they could mess up, who are you to never go wrong?
Although this is the case and we've seen that our opinions and predictions can go wrong, and yes even our hopes can fail us, what really matters is what happens after these errors have been made. Fine, they

got it all wrong and you will also get it totally wrong. The point is, they failed but managed to bounce back and so should you.

So after the errors have been made, do yourself a favour by accepting and letting go. Stop whining and move on. Today Roger Bapson is not very well-known for his wrong prediction on president Hoover, neither is the IMF remembered for their incorrect predictions. We in fact still rely on their forecasts. They did not stop but they continued.

It's usually said that it doesn't help crying over spilt milk. The milk will not go back into the cup, it's already spilt and one must just pour another glass and let go of the spilt cup. Likewise, accept that you were wrong to think or say whatever you did. Stop dwelling on your past mistakes. People may have long forgiven and even forgotten what you did but you're still holding on to it. Until you let it go yourself, you will continue crying over that spilt milk.

So yes, you made a wrong judgement, you thought it was wise to invest in that company when it wasn't, you were deceived into believing that everything would go according to plan and it didn't. Does that change that it all went wrong..? No, it doesn't change a thing. You can't turn back the clock, you can't take back your words but you can choose to change what you can by accepting that mistake and choosing to let it go.

 # YOU CAN GET BACK UP AGAIN – A LESSON FROM THE RAND.

In 2001, South Africa's currency weakened by an astonishing 45% from its strongest to its weakest point against the US dollar. The 2001 September 11 attacks on the World Trade Centre in the USA led the rand to skyrocket to R13.84 to the dollar. The rand had a year average of R8.60 which was its worst level ever. Many thought our currency had collapsed to a point of no return and thought it will never recover from this slump but it did. In 2005, the rand firmed to just over R6.00 to the dollar.

I'm suggesting here that even if you have reached rock bottom, you can get up again just like the rand did. So never give up my friend. As one of the South African rap artists, PROKID said "Ungaphel' Umoya Son" which means don't give up (loosely translated). No matter how rough it is, you have not failed until you surrender. It's not failure if you fall because we all do but its failure if you surrender to the fall and stay down.

As the common saying goes, "it's not over until you say it's over." You haven't failed until you give up all hope. The choice is always yours, to surrender or keep rising after each fall is always up to you. The battle hasn't been lost until you give up and affirm your loss. Therefore, as long as you can still rise and get back up, as long as you're still standing, you haven't given up and you can go on until the victory becomes yours.

No matter how hard you fall, no matter how bruised you get, even though you can no longer walk in a straight up movement, if you keep going, walking and keep standing, you will get back up and move to a place further than you thought you would ever be. You will roll and turn over and stand firm like the rand. So whatever you're going through right now, whether you've fallen or are about to, remember that there's always a chance, opportunity and choice to get back up.

THE DEATH OF A BULL MARKET IS NOT THE BAD NEWS EVERYONE BELIEVES IT TO BE

Contrary to popular belief, when the financial markets 'bullish' state ends, it's usually not as bad as it seems. It's unfortunately coloured much darker than it is because of the tendency to exaggerate the extent and impact of difficulties. Such tendencies have done a lot of damage in making people think that when the bull dies, they won't have anything it once produced for them, neither its meat nor milk. People tend to think that it's all over and the only thing that follows will be financial disasters and poverty.

Jason Zweig once said regarding the end of a bull market, "thanks to the decline in share prices, now is a considerably safer and saner time to build wealth." What a great life lesson this is, even when you're at the lowest point in your life, it's actually not as bad as you think it is. It might actually be the best time to recuperate, build your strategy and execute it well.

Don't give up when you're having your own personal end of a "bull market."

Sometimes the lowest point is actually your greatest. It's your defining moment and it changes your direction. Let's admit it, most of the times we made life-changing decisions, choices that changed our path and placed us into a path of greatness, and choices that made you realise you aren't where you're supposed to be. In most cases, when all such choices were made, it was hardly at the greatest point in our lives.

Look at how death and funerals are the saddest events that put many people at their lowest point yet are also one of the few things that remind us of our mortality. Furthermore, they stimulate the desire to do the right things because all of a sudden we realise how short life is and want to make the most out of it. On the contrary, after the tears are shed and the intense sadness for the grieving fades, they are now fine and go on leading they're usual lives till another funeral comes up.

Unfortunately it usually takes the lowest point for us to reflect and evaluate ourselves and our lives. When we're at the greatest, when all is well and we have no complaints, we tend to think we're doing just fine and we don't need anything more or less. We become too comfortable and settle for where we're at thinking we are perfectly where we need to be. We also tend to loose our ambitions, drive and greater desires.

This is why we need these low points. This is why the bull must die every once in a while. It's so that we can allow the bear to show us how strong we really are. To reveal to us that there's more to life than the bull itself. So when the bull dies, let the bear not only comfort but stretch you. You shouldn't resent the winter and autumn seasons in your life. Remember that seasons change, they alternate, each one comes and goes and it's always for a purpose. Embrace the bear as much as you do the bull, it's always for the best.

It's also worth accepting that life won't always be rosy. Things can be so great right now but we all know it won't always be that great. The point is, the absence of great conditions doesn't have to imply misery. When things seem to fall apart, when nothing seems to be going right, instead of complaining and exaggerating how bad it is when it really isn't, rather keep calm, relax and just let it unfold. Learn all that you need to, open your heart and mind to that experience and let it grow you, make you wiser and stronger.

The reality about life is that you can't apply Avicii's wake me up lyrics. You can't just hope to wake up when it's all over, when you're older and you're stronger. That is not how it works. You experience the bear and go one on-one with it and then you can come out wiser and stronger.

I think this is one of the key points of this book and I can never stress it enough, you must experience the dust in the autumn season and the winter coldness for you to develop as a person. It's a huge and inevitable part of life, that's why bad things happen to the good and bad alike, that's why nobody has a perfect life with forever perfect conditions. It's for our own good so just let it be.

Most importantly, let it teach and grow you because nothing teaches like experience.

Some lessons can only be taught by the worst experiences. Nothing will teach you great lessons like when the rain pours on you and when you're hit by the dusty storm. You really don't have much to learn when it's raining and you're in the house, car or have an umbrella. No matter how hard it pours on you, it can't hurt you if it doesn't affect you terribly. I guess we just like learning the hard way because we never seem to learn much in our summer and spring seasons. I guess it's just too bright and shiny for us to learn.

Another issue or rather paradox is how talking affects us. Talking about our problems really can be therapeutic and indeed it helps. However, the paradox here is that just like overthinking, it also paints our problems darker than they seem.

Suppose that you feel you deserve a promotion at work and Jane gets it instead. You feel a bit sad but later on are happy for Jane and you congratulate her and all that stuff and you get it out of the way. Note that you're genuinely happy for Jane and you feel she also deserves it in any case and there's nothing wrong with her getting the promotion that you really wanted. In your mind and heart, the matter is settled, you're really fine with her getting the promotion and you don't feel it was unfair.

Suppose then that you get home and start thinking about it over and over and start seeing how unfair it was or how undeserving Jane is. You start being negative about the whole situation and can't get it off your mind. In addition, the next morning when one of your colleagues and great work buddy Amy, who knows you really wanted that promotion comes to you and says she understands it can't be easy and you just start blabbing and saying all the negative things you were thinking during your overthinking period. So you release your verbal diarrhoea right there.

You end up talking about how unfair it was and she agrees. You tell her how you're more devoted and would've done a much better job than Jane ever could.

You get home and tell your mother and she says the same thing, go out for dinner with your friends and they all say it. The more you keep talking about it over and over, this thing that wasn't much of a bigger deal when you thought of it at first now becomes a serious issue.

You say all these wrong and negative things and yes you released yourself and all but did it really help? You still don't have Jane's promotion and now you just start hating on Jane, your boss and the company. You're bitter and angry and you can't even enjoy work anymore. All this is the end result of your continuous thinking and overthinking. All because you kept talking and talking and as a result, you built a mountain out of a molehill.

Sometimes we just unnecessarily make this mountain because we exaggerate the severity of the problem. We even loose our own correct perspectives and give in to what others say we ought to feel and think about it. Sometimes all you really need is to individually sit and accept things as they are, to look at things as they are and not see them larger than they really are,

Ask yourself what there is to learn and learn it. By so doing, you'll realise that things aren't as bad as you think. It doesn't have to be a nightmare because it's not a sweet dream. There's always something to learn, even in the midst of the most beautiful spring and summer seasons, open your mind and whenever you're tempted to worry or you start panicking and feeling frustrated, just ask yourself these questions:

- Why am I feeling like this?
- Is it really necessary for me to think, feel or say this?
- What are the chances of this actually happening?
- Am I being realistic or exaggerating things here?
- How can I be more realistic about this situation?

Before you start complaining about your job, think about all the unemployed people out there. There's always a reason to look at the bright side. No dark situation is always just dark. The world is not an awful place, you have lived and are still living in it and you survived and keep surviving. There's always hope and progress.

THE AGENCY PROBLEM

In the financial markets, there's something called the 'agency problem.' The basis of the agency problem is that when senior managers are not invested in the company, they want different results compared to the shareholders. In some cases, what they want may be getting short-term results that may actually jeopardize the company in the long run. This is why most CEOs are now given share options to rectify this.

A solution to the agency problem is basically that the CEO must have shares in the company. When the CEO also has shares, investors become more comfortable to invest in that company. Investors are therefore assured that you want and expect the same things that they do because you're an active participant.

So what do we learn from this? People will not invest in you unless you invest in yourself. Isn't it amazing that some people want others to invest in their dreams yet they wouldn't put their money where their mouths are?

This is why banks don't give loans to just about anybody and even expect collateral. Even business loans require more than just a business plan because people are all talk and confident yet unwilling to put in what they expect others to put in.

So just as much as the bank seeks surety, so will the company you work for, the organisations you belong to and those in your life. Before you ask us for support and to invest in you, you had better be investing in yourself. We need to be assured that you're a valuable investment. Produce as much action as the loud noise you make.

And always ask yourself this: if you had the money and resources or whatsoever you need from others, if you had it all and someone else (you) was in your position of need: Would you invest in you?

"SUCCESS IS THE SUM OF SMALL EFFORTS REPEATED DAY IN AND DAY OUT." R COLLIER

A Quick Lesson on Dividends

Dividends are usually given quarterly in cash from retained earnings. They can be considered a reliable portion of a stock's total return and often reflect the underlying health of a company. In general, companies that grow dividends really benefit more in the long run than those that merely pay dividends (Investopedia Staff, 2009).

For example, one of the findings is that companies that grew their dividends experienced far less volatility (fluctuation/instability) in both the bull and bear markets from 1996 to 2012. On the contrary, companies that cut their dividends during that period were twice as volatile. Therefore, companies that consistently grew their dividends added more value and performed better with less volatility. It's also worth noting that many big companies have high-dividend stocks.

Right, so now that you briefly understand what dividends are and how they work, you need to learn from the markets by realizing that dividend yield is a small component of returns. However, the reinvestment of dividends can compound powerfully and thus create wealth. Likewise, if you keep doing the right thing everyday, in small quantities, success is inevitable.

If you study while others are sleeping, read the right material, work hard everyday, success will come. It might not seem like it at first but remember as long as you are planting the right seeds, you will reap what you sow. We all want to be successful, we all want to make it and be the best in what we do yet very few of us are willing to pay the price. We want all this yet aren't willing to do what it takes to get there. In fact, some don't even know what it takes to get there.

If you want something, you work for it. Hard-work produces success. Nothing will bring itself to you simply because you have the desire and ambition. Similarly, to be successful, as I'm sure most of you want to be is not merely about setting goals, being a big dreamer and going to school. It's more than that, it requires and demands action.

Habits are very significant in our everyday life yet also difficult to cultivate and even more challenging to sustain. I'm sure there are lots of great habits you'd also like to develop for yourself and I'm sure you've tried and probably tried a million times before yet still don't have them cultivated. Hopefully, you're still trying and haven't grown faint because all you really need to do is as they say: do it for over 21 days, well some like exercise are about 3 to 6 months consistently. Furthermore, some like certain virtues may be life-long.

The point here is that success requires consistency in the small little things. Your habits strongly define who you are. Tell me what you can't go a day without and I'll trace it back to how you moved from never doing it- to doing it once- twice and now, most of the time… What you do most says a lot about where you will be in future so if you want success, you practice success on a daily basis through the repetition of small efforts. You're not going to wake up and next thing you know, boom there goes the successful you wrapped in success as the snow covers Japan!

You devote yourself to your work each and every day. You take step-by-step actions each day to develop yourself and the qualities defining and signifying successful people. If it's hard-work, determination and drive, you start now. It must be reflected in the little things you do every day. Just like dividends, these little habits you cultivate each day will sustain you in the long run because they are what will get you where you want to be and beyond that, they will keep you there.

They will sustain you because success doesn't just happen. Remember there is nothing great and strong that can be built in one day. This is why it's significant to be patient and not rush things but to take it one step at a time. Never underestimate small efforts repeated day in and day out. Ask any successful person and they will tell you because this is one of the most significant and imperative ways to make it in any area of your life.

Just like dividends, these small steps may yield small returns but in the long run, you'll see how you could never have survived or been where you are now without them. You can't be spending 80% of your time feeding habits you want to kill. If you want to stop procrastinating and lazing around, you cultivate commitment and diligence right there and then.

You don't wish that someday you'll wake up and the procrastination will be gone. To get rid of such 'success-killing' habits, you don't wait to completely get rid of them but you simultaneously work on the ones you want to develop. When you stop yourself (intentionally and actively) from procrastination, you become more conscious of your actions each day and it may seem futile because it's small steps but one day you'll wake up and it will be almost natural and automatic for you to do it. In those days, you will do what you need/have to do when you need/have to do it without any excuses whatsoever. There'll be no reason or explanation legitimate enough to make procrastination excusable.

Consider what I said earlier about companies that had little dividend growth and put it to practice. They had more volatility, less added value and poor performance particularly when times got rough. Likewise, if you don't grow your 'success habits' you'll experience instability and perform poorly. You bring what you want to see to action by putting a small effort each day. It will greatly benefit and save you in future. It will make things work for you and make them much easier than trying to get it all done and developed in one day.

GET THE PRINCIPLES RIGHT WHEN YOU ARE STILL "SMALL."

Is it not interesting how some people say "when I'm rich like Patrice Motsepe, I will also give half of my money away?" This sounds like a joke to me because honestly, if you can't give away R200, you most probably won't be able to give away R2 million. Certain principles, in fact most principles need to be comprehended whilst you're still 'small.' You must get them settled now before you make it because it may be too late for you to comprehend them later.

In the Johannesburg Stock Exchange, there are companies who are really big as measured by something called market capitalization. Companies such as the British American Tobacco (about R1 Trillion Market Cap), SAB Miller (about R800 billion Market Cap), BHB Billiton (about R600 billion), Richemont (about R400 billion) and MTN (about R350 Market Cap) and very small companies like Hospitality-B with a Market Cap of about R700 million and Petmin with a Market Cap of about R1 billion.

The value of companies rises and falls so when this book is printed, they might have changed but I don't think they would have changed that much. Here's the point, the fact that all these companies are listed on the JSE means they must adhere to strict rules. A company with a Market Cap of R700 million takes governance as seriously as a company with a Market Cap of R1 trillion because of the listing. I'm suggesting that you start taking yourself seriously and establish certain non-negotiable principles in your life right now in your small office, job and company and stop saying you'll start when you're a CEO of a very big company.

I have some non-negotiable life principles of my own that I adhere to: God is important in my life, my family comes second, my work third, my church fourth and everything else after that. So how I spend my time and money is reflected in these priorities. I didn't learn this when I got married or started working. I learned and made these decisions before they were even applicable in my life. I didn't wait for God to do some miracles in my life before deciding He takes priority, I didn't have my own family then but my family always came second and I wasn't really working then but school and my part-time jobs always came third.

I'm just saying that you need to learn and make up your mind before you get there. You don't wait to get there to realise that you shouldn't be choosing work over family. You do it now, at this very moment. If your dream is to be a lawyer, you start acting, speaking and behaving like one before you actually become one. Please don't get me twisted here, I'm not saying you must become your career and even when we have a braai you come in a suit and you always make a case out of our conversations.

All I'm saying is that you make it a point to know what is expected of you before you become a lawyer. You can't be engaging in some criminal activities or smoking weed because you're still doing your third year and you have the whole of next year to quit. You quit now, in fact you weren't even supposed to have started from the beginning. If you've never been one to like suits, you start wearing them once in a while to start practicing. Remember step-by-step. You own a few to make sure you start getting comfortable and like I said, it doesn't mean you start wearing them in unsuitable places.

So get it right before you start. Don't wait to get there because you'll be depriving yourself of one of the key elements in life, preparation. Learn whilst you still have the time, while the pressure isn't too much to handle. This will make it much easier to practice when you're under some serious pressure and you will thrive and not fail. Stop procrastinating and start getting the principles right now while you're still 'small' because you'll master them when you're 'big.'

Many people crumble because they never learned the basics and thus don't know where they stand. Situations force them to make decisions and wrong ones are likely to be made under such circumstances. I just gave you the solution preventing you from being like one of those. The choice is yours to apply or simply listen and do nothing about it until you're forced to and trust me that won't be nice.

You'll seem incompetent and inexperienced, the two qualities people like you shouldn't be displaying. Not just because you're going to a bigger place but because you have this information at your disposal. Use it! If you want to be big, do big, live big, see and practice big while you're still small and you'll be comfortable, competent and experienced by the time you get there. Crumbling will not be an option!

Think about it though, if you can't be trusted in little things, how can you expect to be trusted with much? If you can't manage 50 people, how do you think you can manage 500? The principle remains the same but as the numbers increase, it's easier to manage than when you just begin with 500 because you've learned the challenges and difficulties while you were still small. You have seen what works and what doesn't. You're therefore much wiser, stronger and smarter. So get going, learn and practice the principles whilst you're still small!

 ## "WALL STREET PEOPLE LEARN NOTHING & FORGET EVERYTHING."
BENJAMIN GRAHAM

It was in 2007 when myself and someone I know were in some very serious debt, real debt. We couldn't pay anything and we were in big trouble. We were blacklisted so many times that when someone threatened to blacklist us, we would just laugh it off. I remember our excitement when the country proposed the credit amnesty. This meant that as a country, we would have all default judgements removed from credit bureaus to give people like us a second chance. We took that chance with both hands and that was a lesson learned and never to be repeated.

Mistakes are inevitable, nobody's free from them. I'm sure you've made enough of your own to fill all the pages in this book and more and there's no need to be ashamed. Mistakes are necessary for our growth and have to be made to get us where we need to be. We all know about the wonderful things people say about mistakes, "there's no such a thing as a mistake, it's just a great learning experience."

That may be true and if that's how you choose to see it, great, but unfortunately this is not a feel good about your mistakes chapter so we're not looking into such aspects right now. Moreover, this is not a feel bad about your mistakes section either because the aim is rather to learn and avoid repeating them when we can. I hereby acknowledge the difference among people in the frequency and learning experiences from their mistakes.

The first key thing is that the first mistakes can be excused because that really is experience. But we all know how harsh a teacher experience really is and besides, life's just too short for you to make every mistake possible, so learn from your own mistakes and other people's errors.

"All men make mistakes, but only wise men learn from their mistakes." Winston Churchill

In all that you go through, the worst form of self-disrespect is not learning from your mistakes. If you make the same mistake twice, the first time was definitely futile because you never learned a thing. It might as well not have happened regardless of how sad or painful it must have been. The fact that you didn't grab the lesson means you went through it for nothing other than experience.

Someone I know strongly believes that if you make an awful mistake twice, it's just as good as it never happened because you didn't learn from it the first time. If the experience has taught you a lesson, grab it and make sure the mistake doesn't happen again. Don't be a victim of your errors. Take the lesson and move forward.

You really can't afford to see yourself in a familiar sad place and position. You know when you've been there before. The fact is, as long as you don't learn, you'll walk through the same road a hundred times. You won't move over it until you grab the lesson and move forward so please learn from your errors. If the first investment you made totally backfired and you incurred major losses, you absolutely know to take serious caution next time. You know better because the first experience was harsh and it taught you some great lessons.

This applies well to your personal choices too. if you've walked that road before and you know the reasons why you found yourself in Dark Lane when you were supposed to be in Alice Lane then next time you're on that four-way stop, you'll know which turn to make and which to avoid in order to get to where you're supposed to be (Alice Lane).

The funny thing though is that it's not all that simple. Sometimes we see ourselves go right back to Dark Lane when we know it's seriously dark and how hard it was to get out of there into the bright Alice Lane. We swore we would never cross that path again, we swore it was the last time and we resented being there for longer than we should have yet we still jump right back in.

Why do we do this? Seriously, ask yourself why? Have an honest confrontation with yourself right now about the dark place you keep going back to. Confront yourself and stop blaming anyone or anything and you'll find that answer. You'll find the real reason why you went back and fell into the same deep dark hole twice and even more than thrice for some of you.

After finding the reason, you ought to deal with it, don't brush it off or convince yourself it'll just go away. Sometimes you really have to put up a fight with your navigator to stop taking the wrong turn because it doesn't lead you to where you need or want to be.

Mistakes don't just happen unless we let them. Refuse to let them happen on your watch by honestly evaluating the errors you make and being real and practical to ensure they don't happen again.

Some mistakes are easier to fix than others, some are much more difficult to overcome because of habit and to break the habit, remember to consciously break the thoughts that come with it. If you have a tendency to eat a lot when you're stressed, you don't just tell yourself that next time you get stressed you just won't eat as much because trust me, you will.

The effective strategy here would be to consciously break the association between stress and food by adopting a better stress-coping mechanism that won't cause you weight and health problems. You won't necessarily combat the eating problem but you cultivate another good habit at the same time and slowly but surely, you will get there.

Likewise, if you have a tendency to overspend money, you don't just tell yourself that you'll do better next month. That is so not how it works! You look at what makes you overspend and how you can better overcome it. If it's because you end up buying things you don't need, you draw up a need list, not to merely feel disciplined but to actually put it into practice, otherwise it's all in vain.

The challenge with mistakes is that they get harder to break when they're habitual. Moreover, to attack a habit head on is to be at war, not just with the situation but with yourself. You ought to sacrifice what you think you need for what you really need. You ought to stop the binge-eating when you're stressed because it's not good for you, your body or your health for that matter.

You ought to sacrifice that take-away or outing that you know you can't afford to make sure you don't overspend. Step by step and you'll eventually get there. I'm not saying it will be easy because to overthrow anything in this life is a battle, and to personally overthrow our errors is an even harder battle because it's internal. Therefore, keep fighting and don't let that mistake trap you or make you feel powerless.

What do we gather from all this? All our mistakes have a cause and effect. If you know the cause you can handle the effect and be able to avoid it next time because you're dealing with it from the roots. Lastly, there's always an opportunity to make things right, to recover from wrongs and to come out stronger and better. You aren't trapped, break that pattern. If the road is familiar, you've got to know where to go this time to get the desired outcome.

> **THE INTELLIGENT INVESTOR REALIZES THAT SHARES BECOME MORE RISKY AS THEIR PRICES RISE AND LESS RISKY AS THEIR PRICES FALL."**

This is one the most amazing lessons I've learned from Benjamin Graham and it applies very well to life. When you're at the bottom, you're poor, have no resources, no education and you're broke, there's absolutely no risk of you loosing anything. You really have nothing to loose. However, when you're at the top, successful and have money, you have the risk of loosing it all.

It's easier to get over a short-term relationship than a long-term one because you've been in it for long and invested a lot. It's easier to do foolish things when you're not famous than it is when you are. I'm sure you get it by now. The further you go, even in pursuing your dreams and goals, it gets harder because you've been in it for long. The race, pace and speed gets harder, longer and even more demanding and so do the risks.

That's why you must never be complacent. As the old saying says, "it's easier to get to the top but staying there is another story." Nathan Mayer Rothschild also said it, "It requires a great deal of boldness and a great deal of caution to make a great fortune and when you have got it, it requires ten times as much to keep it."

The higher you go the harder it gets, just like in geography. Don't think because you got there, it's now time to take a chill pill and relax. It's actually time to be cautious because there are more risks when you're on top than when you're at the bottom. Therefore, if you want to go further and further, rest assured that it doesn't get easier and be ready to take more risks and strive to avoid loosing it all.

HUMAN BEINGS ARE LIKE DERIVATIVES: YOUR VALUE DEPENDS ON WHAT HAPPENS TO THE VALUE OF ANOTHER ASSET

Derivatives are financial instruments that derive their value from the values of other underlying variables. Derivatives can be based on almost any variable – from the price of electricity (electricity derivatives), the weather in London (weather derivatives), the creditworthiness of a company (credit derivatives) to the amount of hurricane insurance claims paid in 2003 (insurance derivatives). I'm suggesting human beings are like this; your success is linked to the success of others.

A recent report released by Oxfam (2013) identified South Africa as the most financially unequal place on earth with a gini coefficient (a measure of inequality) of 63.1 which is amongst the worst globally. A Gini index of 0 represents perfect equality, while an index of 100 implies perfect inequality. As it follows from these statistics, 63.1 is a high inequality rate. I would like to assume that this is quite clear in our country, we live in it and see it day-by-day.

Apartheid played a significant role here and the effects are still persistent. We see the division and inequality in terms of class, residence, employment and overall access to resources. Some people are more privileged than others and indeed it does seem that the rich are getting richer and the poor getting poorer. The inequality in South Africa is quite interesting to observe because I keep wondering how these conditions remain the same and how they become perpetuated.

I think it all boils down to the death of the human ethic of care. Whatsoever happened to us that everyone only seems to care about themselves and their own? How do you go by living each day normally when a day hardly goes by without you seeing a hungry person, a beggar and people staying in dreadful shacks? I know these are debatable issues because conditions differ, some are intentional and some are even scams.

However, all I'm proposing is that we start looking at things differently. We are social beings and indeed, just like derivatives we are invaluable without any effect on another variable. So ask yourself this, what good are you if you have no impact whatsoever on those around you? What good is it when the rich and middle class conclude that they will just take their children to private school? What do you think will happen if your child is the only one who has a decent education? Chaos!

I know we all want the best for our children and we want to make sure they succeed but how do we live in a society where the only concern we have is about ourselves and our offspring? What change does this bring? Did humanity really go down the grave with Mother Teresa? Sometimes all they really need is the least valuable thing to you. Kindly help others when and however you can. Touch someone's life and move the attention from yourself, just this once.

I once saw a Facebook picture that depicted a very malnourished child and the message said "The world's hunger is getting ridiculous. There is more fruit in a rich man's shampoo than in a poor man's plate." This may seem like an exaggerated analogy but I believe there's some truth to it. The problem with our modern society is that we are forever in want and it's always about getting more and more.

Success is about how much one has, it's about the cars, the house, the expensive products they use and the ridiculously costly clothes they wear. If you can afford it, fine, there's nothing wrong with that but do you really need all that? Do you really have no better things to spend your money on? What about the welfare of others? I think these are some the questions our minds have grown strange to because we are too self-absorbed and care too much about material possessions. We rely too much on materials to define us and that's why we spend so much on them.

Nothing is ever good enough yet what we have for breakfast is more than enough for the poor man's full day meal. What we call our ragged clothes are good enough to wear to a very special event for some. I'm just asking that we stop wanting and start caring.

Honestly, some of the things we possess are really unnecessary.

If the world was a better place, if people were more equal, then maybe it would be okay but not in South Africa. We are not in America here, stop living the American dream when your fellow South Africans are dying of poverty! But then again, these are just my thoughts…

"PRICE IS WHAT YOU PAY, VALUE IS WHAT YOU GET." WARREN BUFFET

A few years ago I often used plumbers, electricians and carpenters that I could pick up from a certain corner in our neighbourhood. I often used them because I thought I was getting 'value for money.' My thinking was: why should I pay professionals when I can get someone else to do the same work at half price? When I saw this quote by Warren Buffet, I started asking myself if I was really getting value from these guys.

As I pondered on this, I realised that whenever I needed their services, I had to skip work to pick them up, take them to buy whatever they need to use from the stores and I was basically too involved. Furthermore, I incurred some major loses for missing work. So when my wife decided to do some minor renovations, we decided to use professionals and that's when I understood what 'value' meant. We paid a relatively high amount compared to our friends from the corner but great value is what we got.

In the modern society, there is what we call consumerism where people are encouraged to get informed and demand value for their money because they paid for the service. This gives consumers the right to question, suggest and demand good service. People with expertise thus take consumers seriously and do an outstanding job. However, you can only do this if you're willing to pay. Pay the price and get the value, simple as that.

So my friend, don't cut corners, pay professionals to do the work and you'll understand the true meaning of 'value.' People will pay you very well if you create value for them. As professional speakers people often ask: why should I pay you so much money to speak for only an hour? The answer is always: you don't pay me for the hour but for the value I bring to the hour. What value do you bring at your workplace or to your clients?

CHANGE YOUR WORDS AND CHANGE YOUR WORLD.

This is something I've been living with for the past 13 years. I remember every time I went to the township I was born in at Soweto and I'd find some of the guys I grew up with sitting under a tree saying things like "sisokola sonke" meaning, we're all struggling/battling/trying because times are tough. Whenever they said this I always used to say, no dude, I'm not battling with you. Even though I didn't have the money then, I said the right and positive things about myself. I refused to paint a poor present and future for myself.

I refused to engage in those pity-parties because I understood that there's something about what you say about yourself that can attract either the positive or negative. If you keep putting yourself down and doubting your ability and capabilities, you will be the exact limitation you place on yourself. Everyone will keep discrediting and disqualifying you because that's what you do to yourself in any case.

Talking may appear to be an automatic process that happens without our conscious awareness but it's not. Think about when you were still a toddler and started learning how to talk. Nobody came here talking. We were all born without words in our mouths and we never really knew what and when to say it until we reached a certain age. The mistake that we make is thinking that things are different because we are adults and know how to talk.

We stop analysing what we say, we remove our awareness from how we talk and just do it because it's a norm. This somehow gets us loosing the wisdom to grasp the power of words. When we were still toddlers, most of the words we uttered were for a purpose and mostly because we were told to say it. Our parents taught us to call them 'mama' and 'papa' and it may not have sounded perfect the first time but we eventually got it and said it perfectly. This shouldn't change because we are now adults. The words we speak shouldn't be some normal thing we do without thinking, selecting and reflecting.

This is not just about how we talk to others but also about how we talk to ourselves and the situations we are in. We should be very careful of what we say and not just look into why we said it. You may not realise it but your words really shape how you see yourself, others and the world you live in. We don't realise this because we tend to be oblivious to the fact that our words reflect what goes on within us.

They reflect what we think about and how we think about it and that's why it's important to not just change your words but change your mind whilst you're at it. This is a simultaneous process because the mind and mouth work hand in hand. Let me use an example here. Say Jacob has a very low self-esteem, he's always falling behind on his work and most of his days can be classified as unproductive. So Jacob really needs help here and is told by his therapist to look at himself in the mirror every morning and say "I am strong, confident, intelligent and I'm going to have a very productive day." Jacob may say it the first time for the sake of saying it and may continue because it's habitual even though he knows it's not really true because things are still the same no matter how much of this he says. In this case, it can be seen that Jacob has merely changed his words and not his mind. However Jacob might just be saying it so much he actually starts believing it and starts saying it with more zeal and truth the next time.

Alternatively, say during the early stages when Jacob used to say it without believing, let's say his therapists realised this and told him to engage in some cognitive restructuring and consciously work on believing and making it more personal, real and true to himself. The next morning, Jacob says it but this time he actually believes it, he says each word about three times until he believes it's true and eventually starts seeing himself like that. It can be seen in this case that Jacob changed his mind and yet said the same words yet this time with more substance because he believed it and the change followed.

So now let's take you, yes you, the person reading this book right now. Every word you say is not automatic, you say it because you think it and you think it because you believe it. If you have a negative perception about yourself, your boss, your boring miserable life, whose fault is that? How are you thinking about all this and what are you saying about it? If you continuously complain and say all these negative things to yourself or to others, you start believing it and it will colour how you see your world. So whether your world is green, black or yellow depends largely on what you say about it.

Think about this, sometimes things aren't as dark as they seem until you start thinking about it as problematic. If you keep thinking about it that way over and over and long enough, trust me you'll eventually see it that way. Even though they were just cream white, our words can turn them into pure white and even if they were just grey, our words can turn them into the darkest black. Moreover, our words can also turn white into black and the opposite is also true. This is just a colour analogy to show how the way we see our world is shaped by the words we speak.

So if you want change in your world, don't forget to change your words too. Now, the colour analogy might have simplified this but remember it doesn't change a thing if you're merely going to say things differently when you don't actually believe it. Don't cheat and deceive yourself like that, don't lie to yourself, be real and honest to yourself if not to others.

Merely changing your words will not necessarily change reality unless your words are true and you're actually working to change that reality. So what am I saying? I'm not saying you must go around saying 'I drive an X5' when you drive a Tazz and that Tazz will turn into an X5. No, I didn't say that. Not guilty!

All I'm saying is that you must realise how your words shape the way you see things and therefore alter them to see things differently. Sometimes all you need is a positive evaluation or highlight of that negative situation. You can therefore use a different approach, different words and tone to say the same negative thing and it won't sound so negative.

It's really possible to give criticism without making anyone feel belittled and ridiculed. It's therefore possible to give some major criticisms and still have the person confused or unsure as to whether that was a criticism or a minor correction. You can say the wrong thing in the right way. What determines the effect is the change in your approach.

Whilst we still on the subject of words, it's also important to not only watch what we say to ourselves about us or our worlds but also watch what we say to others. Unfortunately people judge us according to what we say so we must be careful in choosing the words that come out of our mouth, especially since we can't even take them back. Words can hurt and heal, break and fix and show love or hate. Words have power that we can't afford to take for granted. Friendships, relationships and even marriages have been built and destroyed by words. One wise or foolish word can get you that business deal or make you get loose it. Think about the many things that went wrong simply because people didn't address you or you didn't address them properly.

Think about how if the correct words were used, things would have turned out differently and you'll see that words aren't just automatic and neutral language terms but powerful and effective. Words can do so much for you, good and bad alike. But if words are to do anything for you, it's obviously better if it's for your good and gain.

So let's stop putting other's down but instead tell them we believe in them, let's affirm instead of breaking down others. Be the reason someone smiles today, it doesn't have to cost you a thing. You don't even have to buy them a gift, just tell them you believe they can do it, tell them they look nice today, and tell them they have a beautiful smile or voice. All these smiles for the cost of R0.00 because all it takes is just a few kind, gentle words from your mouth, nothing out of your pocket.

EXCEPTIONALLY HIGH EARNINGS AND GROWTH RATES ARE UNSUSTAINABLE

There is no company that can sustain exceptional high growth rates for too long (Franco Busetti). The truth is if your company is growing at say 20% per annum for a long period, a new entrant will be attracted to your industry and will moderate your company's growth rates.

Even as human beings, steady growth rates are always better. Those who rise to leadership and prominence too quickly are in a risk of falling as quickly. You can't always take the short and easy way out. There is something called premature exposure. Getting certain positions too quickly can kill the great potential you have as a human. Don't be too hasty.

With such things as wealth and success, it's very clear that they shouldn't be rushed because they will crush you when attained prematurely or through dodgy schemes. Think about it, how many get-rich-quick schemes have succeeded? How many people who fell for these are still rich today?

As I said in the chapter on success, you don't just wake up successful and likewise, you won't wake up wealthy. Only criminals and schemers do that which I'm sure you're not, so work and go through all that you need to. Don't try to fast-track your growth because you will crash, it's just not sustainable. What you gain quickly, you will also loose quickly so work to make it happen and stop settling for quick processes that won't sustain you. Choose to be sustainable, avoid rushing things and patiently endure the process of getting there.

PRICING POWER IS DERIVED FROM DIFFERENTIATION, NOT BY BEING A COMMODITYBUSINESS – YOUR TALENT IS YOUR MONEY

Pricing power is the effect that a change in product price has on the quantity demanded. When companies change their product prices, the change in price can result in either more or less of the product demanded. Pricing power can therefore be regarded as the extent to which a company may raise prices without reducing its demands for the product.

In general, a company that offers a unique product or has few competitors because of its uniqueness and quality of service typically has strong pricing power. Therefore, it may raise prices without reducing the product's demand. If a company doesn't have much pricing power, then an increase in their prices would reduce the demand for their products. This applies to life as well; your value depends on your uniqueness and quality.

It's really about what and how much you can offer. Just like pricing power, if you aren't unique then you're just like everyone else and there's no significant difference between you and your competitors. It takes uniqueness to stay on top and win over everyone else. This uniqueness is found in each and every one of us, that's why it's very significant that we always be ourselves and stick to who we are. Let everything that you do radiate who you are, let it have your natural essence.

We all have a personality that may be similar to others but the essence differs. We all have unique talents that we're born with. Sadly some people never know what they are, some never invest in them and still others never use them to their full capacity. I hope that you're not one of those because your talent is your money.

Learn from the markets, the ability to raise prices is one of the most fundamental characteristics that investors analyse when doing research on companies. Likewise, your talent is your treasure, if you want to raise your price, invest in it and put it to good use. The key determinants of pricing power of a good service include its uniqueness, competition, effectiveness, quality and performance in the markets. The more a company possesses these elements, the higher the pricing power.

Similarly, the more you stick to who you are and to utilizing your talents, the more of these elements you have. You become effective, produce quality, perform on merit and win the competition. All this happens when you stick to who you are because you're the best when you're you. Dare to be different, dare to be you and use your talent to raise your own pricing power.

"IF YOU ARE BORN POOR IT IS NOT YOUR FAULT BUT IF YOU DIE POOR IT IS." BILL GATES

Nothing expresses the power of choice as the above statement does. Nobody chooses where they come from or where they're born. No-one can be blamed for being born into a poor family. We can excuse it. However what cannot be excused is blaming the life circumstances one was born into for them being poor their entire lives. How many people do you know who were the first to go to university in their family? How many rich people, millionaires and even billionaires do you know who were born poor?

If you aren't an alien and live in the world that I live in, chances are, you know tons of people who had it rough yet are now very rich and successful. Think about people like Richard Maponya, Herman Mashaba and the likes. Bring it close to home and think about the people you know who were born and raised under some very difficult circumstances yet made it out on top. These people that you know aren't special in any way. They just never made excuses so you also can't afford to. They didn't blame the government or the system for the circumstances they were in but instead chose to take charge and bring about the change they wanted to see.

There is therefore no difference between you and them. We all come through life the same way (birth) and exit in the same manner (death), we all have 24 hours per day and the freedom of choice to use those 24 hours every day. The only thing that differs is who you're born as and where you're born but in general, we all have a choice to determine whom we'll die as. If they could do it, so can you and any other person you know who was born and raised in extreme poverty.

Poverty cannot be an excuse anymore, not in this day and age. True, rich and wealthy people have more opportunities, connections and resources that the poor person doesn't have. However, isn't it interesting how although this is the case, it has never stopped anyone poor from rising above the limitations and obstacles that come with their life circumstances? Now, don't get me wrong, I'm not saying we should start playing some silly blame game with poor people because if you don't know poverty, it might be easier to say 'they got themselves into this mess.'

Food for Thought

Indeed, poverty can be overcome but we must be sensitive as to what we say to and about the poor. The sad thing about poverty is that it's not just a material and physical state but some form of mental captivity and slavery, which is more difficult to break than the physical. What being poor does is that it focuses on immediate satisfaction and needs and so it's more difficult to say go to school (12 years) and varsity (another 3-4 years) then you'll see the change.

If I'm poor and you tell me to wait for pretty much 15-16 years of my life so I can have better living conditions and an improved standard of living, I'd tell you that's a waiting period I don't have because honestly, it might sound cliché but life is what happens while we're busy making other plans.

The poverty is there NOW, I face it every day NOW and each day I struggle and strive to make ends meet so I don't go to bed on an empty tummy. Some of you might not even know what that's like yet are so quick to blame them for having 5 kids when they saw a way out in it, for being prostitutes when all they saw was a way out for their young ones, for being the annoying street vendors in the streets of Joburg who all sell the same thing when what they saw was a way to ensure that their kids get the opportunity to wear new clothes for Christmas like the kids next door.

The truth is, we seem to claim that we know a lot about why people are poor and why they aren't doing something about it when we wouldn't even survive an hour in their shoes. In a society where so much of our identity, value and worth is judged by the area you live in, the size, shape and design of your house, the car you drive and the stores you buy food and clothing, we ought to be more sensitive to the poor because it must be the most embarrassing thing to have your identity and value attached to the shack you live in, the food you don't have and the clothes you can't afford!

So much is prescribed for us in this modern age. We are told that success is based on the car you should have, the mansion you should be staying in and the Woolies food you should be eating. We even forget we aren't the cars we drive at times because so much of our identity is tied to it. All I'm saying is that poverty is not as clear-cut as it seems and we need to be a bit more considerate in how we address and talk about such issues and thus I'm tackling it with sensitivity here.

Moving On…

Right, so I may not know who you are or where you're reading this right now. You might be in the comfort of your big comfortable bed or couch or maybe you don't even have either of those but I tell you this: right now, at this very moment, you have the choice to break free and make a different choice. Remember you can't want a different life yet still make the same old choices. Set your mind free first because no matter how much money you can get, if your mind is still entrapped, your freedom will be nothing more than a temporary state.

Choose to think and do things differently. If you want to get out of anything, you work not just walk your way out. The same is true for poverty, no-one is an exception, you must work your way up. If it's school that you need, go study, if business would work for you then go get serious, learn about it, get that business proposal and get that business running. Whatever it is, take some form of action. No more excuses, no more pity-parties. Get up and go do whatsoever you need to get out. Go accomplish it, make it work for you and you'll see the change.

People may tell you how won't make it because no-one in your family ever did. They might not see any potential in you. They may confine you to who you were born as and where you were born and you can't change that. You can't change what they'll think or say about you, it's a human condition. The biggest mistake you could ever make is to see yourself as they see you.

Never get your reality picture get painted by people who have no idea of who you are and what you've been through. What matters most is indeed what you say about you and to you, not what they say. It's how you see and think about yourself, not their blinded vision and ridiculous thoughts that matters.

If they can't see you beyond your poverty, shack, cleaning job or level of education, the worst you can do is assist them. It really can't benefit you to be pulling yourself down when they already are. You and only you have the power to decide how the story will end. You determine the ending and it could be either happy or sad but it's all up to you. You have the pen in your hand, write your ending as you see fit. No limitations, no boundaries, no confinements and absolutely no restrictions. Not from your current or past life circumstances and definitely not from 'them.' We all have 'them' you know yours and the power they have to determine your present and future is the power you have given them.

IF IT WORKS FOR SOMEONE ELSE, IT DOESN'T MEAN IT WILL WORK FOR YOU

There are several companies in the JSE that provide unsecured lending, also known as personal loans (I'm trying to be fancy, you see). I want to use two of these companies to illustrate a point. These are: Blue Financial Services LTD and Capitec Bank Holdings LTD. These companies are big in the unsecured lending space but their fortunes are quite interesting.

In 2013, Capitec released very good results and Blue Financial Services actually announced that they are exiting the unsecured lending market. Isn't this interesting? Just because it's good for someone, even though they're doing the same things you're doing doesn't mean it will work for you. Therefore, follow whatever it is that works for you.

Perhaps one of the problems with modern society is the exposure that we have to each other's lives through social media. This is where most people choose to just display their TMI (Too Much Information) syndrome. People tell you what they're doing and all about their successes. This is where you find a lot of prescriptions about how to do this and that, what works and doesn't work. This is a great arena because you can get some good advice and tips and that's why you ought to be open-minded and learn from others.

However, these prescriptions aren't like doctor's prescriptions. They don't really understand your health; they don't know what you need or what's best for you. That's why you don't just take any of these and put them into practice. You choose what works and doesn't work for you because what works for Siphiwe won't necessarily work for Sipho. These are two different people with two different destinies, abilities and gifts. That's why comparison and competition with others is never healthy.

We may be going the same direction, our paths may seem similar but as they say, there are over 50 ways to kill a cat and over a 1000 ways to die. These all have a similar end yet the route is not the same. Learn from this, just because you want to get into business doesn't mean you must get into franchise because McDonalds is doing very well or your friend just bought some KFC store and business is great. You shouldn't go off to pursue it just because it worked for him. You might be more successful at events planning than franchising.

So do what works for you. Do what corresponds to your passion, likes, goals, personality, gifts and abilities. These obviously differ from person to person; even twins don't take the same path. In the end, you're an individual; you are you and not he or she. Let the competition and comparison come to an end today as you do what you do best. No matter how big or small, just do you. Not all of us are going to be CEO's and there's nothing wrong with that. Just be you and do what you love and you'll have your peace and serenity.

It's better to be "small" in what you love and are destined for than to continuously toil to be "big" in someone else's path. I'm not saying some people are more prone to success than others, I'm just saying there are different ways and levels to go about it. Some people have the smallest yet successful businesses, they master what they do and happily do it. They are comfortable with what they get out of it, well at least until they start focusing too much on comparing themselves and competing with someone else's business.

The reality is, some people study 3 hours to get 90s and others study 10 hours to do the same. Some sleep 4 hours to recuperate and be more productive and still others need 10 hours to function at that similar level. Some good musicians went to music school and still other great musicians didn't. None is better than the other. We are just wired differently.

We have different needs and our minds work differently. We are affected and influenced by different things. We may all be from rich or poor families but we all have different outcomes. Before you start feeling small by comparison, always remember that. Before you start taking advice, tips and prescriptions, think about how everyone went through a totally different experience from you to get to where they are.

Save yourself from all the unnecessary burden of strife, envy and jealousy by accepting today that your path is not theirs and similarly, theirs is not yours. What works for you might never work for anyone else and likewise, what works for everyone else may never work for you. Be the best you can be by doing what suits and works for you. It doesn't make it wrong, less meaningful or insignificant because it's not what Ophrah did.

INVESTING IN YOURSELF, JUST LIKE INVESTING IN THE STOCK MARKET, IS CHEAPER THAN YOU THINK

When I was 26, I registered for an MBA and because I was 'too junior' in my company to qualify for a bursary to study for an MBA, I paid for it myself, well, at least for the first two years. When I told some people, they said it was too expensive and asked how I was able to afford it. The very people wore some really expensive shoes and paid about R2, 000 a month on clothing accounts from a net salary of around R4, 800. I was paying about R2, 000 per month as well for my education.

The same happens with investments. People often say the stock market is too expensive when in fact "Brokerage charged by stockbrokers varies from 0.35% to 1.70% of the value of the transaction" (Stock Exchange Handbook, 2013). People say this is expensive, yet they pay about 20% fees on some credit cards and sometimes about 30% costs on some unsecured loans. So in the end, who's fooling who?

You can see here that indeed investing in yourself is cheaper than you think and contrary to popular belief, investing in the stock market is also cheaper than you think. It's really important that you start investing your time, money and other resources in yourself because it always pays off. And besides, if you're not investing in yourself who will?

Unfortunately we live in a world where everything is about using what you have and always focusing on our immediate needs. That's why I would say if you're not investing in yourself then your investment is elsewhere, somewhere it shouldn't be. Sadly most of us aren't even taught how to invest for the future and honestly, there's no better way to do that that investing in you.

You're the only person that knows you best and you're a worthwhile investment. Investments may fail you but you cannot afford to fail yourself so invest in yourself. We'll call it a personal, person-centred investment. It's personal because it's about you and person-centred because you're the master of your investment.

I'm sure you know the areas in which you need growth and development. You most probably know what you need to do to get to the place you want to be and become the person you want to be. Determine your action plan today and put it to action. Remember just like dividends, your personal investment determines whether you'll stand or crumble in volatility because throughout the fluctuations, you'll stand because you'll get the returns of your dividends (small personal investments).

Cultivate the virtues, do what you need to, it's cheaper to invest in yourself. As the saying goes, if you think education is expensive, try ignorance. In addition to that, the returns are always for your benefit. You really have nothing to loose but everything to gain.

DON'T PANIC OVER PRICE CHANGES

Share prices go up and down every day but investors must chill and not panic as long as they have a long-term view. This in my view is Life 101, life goes up and down but we should never panic as long as we're going somewhere. Relaxation is one of the key things in life yet has lost value in these hectic modern days. We panic because we make lots of plans and expect all of them to work out and when some of them don't, we force them to work and drain ourselves until they do.

When things change and aren't the way we're used to, by the time we reach a state of relaxation, we've sadly had 10 mini heart-attacks because of the anxiety that comes with not knowing what's happening. We want things to be familiar and return to a state of equilibrium. What we need to learn here is that there's nothing wrong with not knowing. You don't always have to know or understand what's going on. It's okay if you don't, one day you will. Think about the many things you never knew of until they happened to you. You must have freaked out at first but you know how to handle it well today.

Life is like the primary market (a market for new issues or new financial claims). The things in the primary market happen for the first time and are unknown to the public before they are issued. When change happens and things that are unknown to us happen for the first time, innovation is key. You need to find new ways of dealing with the unknown.

The secondary market on the other hand is regular because it has long passed the primary market stage. It's continuous and generally a norm. In this case, some things don't need to be changed because things have been working out well as they have been. What makes us panic in life is pretty much the primary and not the secondary market because it's new and unknown and therefore uncomfortable. That's why we need to know that what is new is not necessarily harmful. Change that association.

When change happens and you feel uncomfortable, sometimes all you really need is either adopt a new strategy or let things go on as they normally have been. Sometimes change feels so uncomfortable that we want to change even that which is unnecessary. If you're an authoritative parent for example, the loving and caring yet strict type, when your children mess up, you don't have to turn into a monster parent and be authoritarian by controlling them, bossing them around and withdrawing your affection. Sometimes you must just discipline them in the same way, with a strict tone yet with love and they will be corrected.

In general, when change occurs because things have gone wrong, it's an opportunity to grow and make things right. Suppose you've been planning a major event and an important artist drops you in the last minute. The natural response here will be panic, fear and disappointment. Suppose also that there happens to be a much younger upcoming artist which you could've conveniently asked before but didn't.

Realizing what's happening, she volunteers to perform. You're obviously skeptical as you've always been about her but have no choice so you let her. To your amazement, the audience loves her, she engages them and keeps them cheerful and jolly. They are completely blown away and the event is rated 10 out of 10 because of her awesome performance.

You can see here that there's always an opportunity to recover from wrongs and come out better and stronger. A change of plans doesn't have to freak you out. Sometimes it's for your own good and just what you need. Change therefore gives an opportunity to comprehend things differently. It makes growth possible because sometimes all we need to get out of the comfort zone is some kick of the primary market. It's when we're out of the comfort zone that we're most able to expand our horizons.

In the financial markets which I believe you're now familiar with, risks and fluctuations are inevitable and there are no guarantees. This is how we ought to think of life because change works in the same manner. Change is inevitable and nothing is ever guaranteed to go as planned so when change happens, instead of being fearful and uncomfortable rather allow yourself to grow or else you'll remain stagnant. Change should amuse us instead of paralyzing us with fear because of the growth it brings.

We know very well that the future is not always predictable and no method of technical analysis (method of attempting to predict future changes) can ever be too exact to make a perfect prediction. Therefore even in your future plans, remember to include the probable change. Some of you want to study law, some of you are really enjoying your LLB course right now and some of you are lawyers yet all of this might not have been part of the plan and only happened because of change.

What you're really passionate about today may not be your passion tomorrow and what you really wanted to do may not be what you're supposed to be doing. Change is inevitable and you must always be conscious of this. Things will not always be as they are and will not always turn out as planned and that's okay!

No matter how disturbing the change feels, even if it's not working in your best interest, keep your focus. Don't just see the now but look beyond it. What was once new can become regular. There's always a move from the primary to the secondary market. Adjust in times of change and start getting comfortable because it won't always be unsettling.

You cannot wait for conditions to be comfortable or pleasant for you to do what you need to do. You cannot wait for the change to be over before you continue living or take action. Keep moving even if the fear that comes with change is there. Rather do it when you're afraid than do nothing until things calm down. Keep your focus and keep pursuing your goals even if change makes it uncomfortable.

My advice is this, if you know the cause, you can handle the effect. If change is the cause of your uncomfortable state then you can handle whatever it brings. Be open-minded, willing to lean and ready to grow. If not, trust change to push you there! Don't wait for the hard kick, don't panic when it strikes, keep calm and adjust to change. Get used to it.

EXPERIENCE ALWAYS COUNTS

In the financial markets, volatility means the fluctuation period. When volatility is high, there can be a sudden and drastic change in price and when volatility is low, there's a steady and gradual change of price. It is possible to make money from volatility but this should not be attempted by first time investors. In general, high volatility is a much more risky period to invest especially for new investors. Experienced investors on the other hand use volatility to their advantage by buying more of what is cheap and selling more of what is expensive (Idris Seedat, 2013).

This was just to illustrate the point that there are different ways to play the same game for the experienced and inexperienced players. As it can be seen here, experience always counts. Financial markets, particularly the cash market is intricate and should be handled with great caution. Because of its nature, experienced traders are the key players as opposed to the inexperienced.

The same principle applies to life. You cannot just get into things you know nothing about. And if you really want to get into them, get the required knowledge before you make any drastic decisions. Life is fun and adventurers and it's always good to take some risks, try out new things and do what you've never done before. However, life is also not a game. You don't gamble with it because you can or feel like it. You take wise and cautious risks not foolish ones.

If you're an experienced investor, you know how the market works. You know which risks are worth taking and which to avoid. You understand that there are no guarantees and things might not go according to plan. This is why managers and other people in major positions need to be more experienced. People in such positions need to understand how things work and must have been there long enough to know how it all operates.

That's why inexperienced people cannot hold such positions. They freak out when things don't go according to plan. Many things take them by surprise and they aren't sure how to respond or what they should do. They mostly learn on a trial-and-error basis. In the markets, there's no space for trial-and-error. Frequent errors will empty your pockets and leave you broke. That's why you need to understand and be exposed to the markets before you do anything.

Experienced investors are like managers and the elderly, they know how to adapt to the inconsistent changes and how to cope even when the wind blows to an unexpected direction. They know things will not always go as planned. They know how to prepare for the future because their experience has given them the necessary and required exposure.

Experience really is the best teacher. Nothing will teach you like it because it's first-hand. However, in life you obviously won't experience everything and some things are for your own good. You don't have to experience how hot and severe the fire is when you saw your friend burn from it. Learn from other people's experiences and don't make the same mistakes. That's why it's important to listen to the elders. The fact is, they've been more exposed to life and people than you have. They have seen and experienced things you never even knew existed.

They may be frail and have grey hair but these people possess abundant wisdom. They know that some things are never as they seem. They know how people operate and have good judgement. They cannot be easily swayed and manipulated. The inexperienced on the other hand are more susceptible to the intricate market. They fall for the so called 'perfect investments' because it seems perfect. They are not very analytical and may fall for the buzzwords because they don't have much experience.

They have not seen much and do not understand how sudden the prices can change. As a result, Experience always counts in the favour of the experienced because they have seen some tough times and endured them. They have made mistakes and learned from them.

In sum, expertise requires experience. You can have all the qualifications in the world but you're of little use without some real hands-on experience. Don't tell us what you have, tell us what you've done and what you can do. Get up and get yourself exposed. If you want to get into business, go experience the business world. If you want to be a singer, get exposed to the music world. Whatever it is you want to get into, get up and take action. Go get your experience, expose yourself!

WHEN WE SEE A GAME, THEY SEE BUSINESS

Michael Jordaan, the former Chief Executive of First National Bank was recently announced as the Chairman of MXIT. When I told someone this story, they asked me whether I meant the same MXIT he spent so much time on and I said yes. He was so surprised that someone could leave FNB to join MXIT. He actually didn't even know that it was a business. I then used the opportunity to chat to him about Alan Knott-Craig Jnr who also left as the CEO of MXIT to start another ambitious project called Project Isizwe aimed at having free Wi-Fi in Africa.

Another Captain of Industry who left a big organization to start a small company is Mark Lamberti, former CEO of Massmart Holdings. Marks' story is interesting because he's the founder of Massmart. He took it to become a 28 000 employee business and then quit to start Transaction Capital in 2012 which already has revenues of about R5 billion. The point is this: when we see a game, a platform to chat, upload pictures and all that, other people see real business. Look around you. Is there any business idea you're missing? Some people are constantly on a look out for business, are you?

People are complaining about their boring jobs and unemployment yet tons of businesses are waiting to be established. Open your mind to see beyond how things appear. It's amazing how powerful the human mind is yet some of us never seem to put it to work. Opportunities never seize to exist, let your mind, knowledge and talent work for you.

Note of Caution: even though this is the case, starting a business is not all that easy. If you think working for your boss or company is hard, starting your own business is most probably 10 times more and we're not all cut out for it so I'm not saying everyone should just go start a business now. If you have the idea, plan and resources and you know it's what you want and can absolutely do it, then go for it. Just don't expect it to be a walk in the park!

DELAYED GRATIFICATION

"You can pay now and play later, or you can play now and pay later. But either way, you are going to pay" John C. Maxwell. Many people just think life is a game, they are always playing and not paying the price for success through learning, working, being mentored etc. They want short cuts, they want that car now, that house now, everything is now; they just can't wait.

I really love what Melanie Senter Lubin, securities commissioner for the State of Maryland in the US said about some of the phrases you should be careful of from your financial adviser. These include: "Don't you want to be rich" "There's no downside" "Trust me" "You will be sorry if you don't" "It's a no-brainer" "We can beat the market" "You need to hurry" "The opportunity of a life time" "You can't afford not to own it" "You can't loose" and "I'm putting my mother in it."

"IF SOMEONE PROMISES YOU A DEAL WITH THESE PHRASES, RUN." Why? Because nothing ever comes that easy no matter how great it sounds! There are no shortcuts to being rich. Wealth is built. The easier it sounds, the greater the danger so be careful of the buzzwords. As they buzz around your ears, don't let them determine your action, don't even let their buzz sound like a sweet melody. It should rather be an irritation to your ears because they will only derail you if you follow through.

I'm certain that one of the key things emphasized and learned in this book is that you work your way up and nothing worthwhile is easily attained. Avoid these shortcuts because they aren't worth it. It's one thing to know and take a short-cut to Durban and another to follow a short-cut in life. The former is great because it'll get you there faster and simpler. It'll save you petrol and a make a long journey shorter.

However the latter will destroy you. It will take whatever you've built and put it into ruins. You will take all that you have and invest in a get rich quick scheme and loose it all in the blink of an eye. Indeed, not all that looks glitters is gold. It may look, feel and shine like it but in the inside may not be. Don't just hear and listen to these buzzwords, there aren't such easy deals in the markets, not even in life. You cannot seriously base your decisions on a nice melody to your ears. Be very careful of that.

You need to think about it, question and analyse it and rather play the skeptic than fall into a trap because the melody was just too nice. Rather delay your temporary wealth by building a stable permanent one even though it takes 10 years more than the former because in the end, it will be worth it.

Whatsoever is laboured for is always worth it. Think about the difference between inheritance and money that was laboured for. The former is easier to misuse because the person doesn't really know what and how much it took to build it whereas the latter is valuable because there was hard labour and sacrifice to attain it. Nothing ever comes while you're sitting. What you sacrifice today will get you a better tomorrow. Think about where you are now. You are there because of every little choice and action you took or didn't take. If you were out partying while the others were busy studying, it's nobody's fault that you failed the module. Moreover, if you only started preparing a few days before while you were chilling the whole semester, the consequences are yours to face.

The point is, other students sacrificed the partying, watching that series and many other things they could have been doing. It's not that they had nothing better to do. They chose to delay their gratification and do what they had to do instead and now they have passed and are done with that module. They got the rewards of their labour and so have you. You will reap the fruits of your harvest.

Similarly, if you work smart and hard, save, avoid debt, invest and make use of the opportunities and resources presented to you, you will reap the fruits of wealth. It may not be 2 years from now, not even 10 but it will happen because you invested. You delayed your desires to get rich quick and chose to work for it. Your wealth will be stable and sustainable. Choose to labour for your future, it is never in vain.

It may look like there's no point right now but it will make sense when you reap the rewards. You always have to put in something to get something out. Even Outsurance expects its clients to pay before they can cover them. So today ask yourself this, what instant gratification are you delaying? Before you start hating on us for our success, before you start thinking we're involved in some scams and tenders, remember we delayed our instant gratification to get where we are.

It wasn't easy and it never is but we chose to. Don't be pointing fingers when we finally get our results because you were chilling while we were toiling. You can't expect what you didn't put in. You can't go to the ATM when you know there's nothing in there and expect money to come out. If it wasn't there it will not be there. If you never put it in, you will not withdraw it. There is no silver platter served if you never toiled and sacrificed like the rest of us.

STOP LYING; YOU ARE NOT SELF-MADE

Benjamin Graham, Philip Fisher, John Burr Williams and Charles Munger. There's a high probability that you don't know these people but you know Warren Buffet don't you? He's arguably the world's best investor and all the people I've mentioned here are said to have taught him a lot of what he does today, both formally and informally (Robert Hagstrom). This goes to show that all of us learn from others.

No-one should dare claim that they are who and where they are because of their own intelligence or effort. You may have made it now but remember the parents and grannies, the aunties and uncles who were involved in your life and did for you what you could not do for yourself. They fed, bathed, dressed and took you to the nursery. When you had no say and not much of a brain and your body was still small and weak, they nurtured you.

Remember the parents and family who took you to school for the first time, before you even knew what the degree you keep crediting for your success was. Yes we get it, you're the one who studied and worked hard, all credit to you but you are not where you are solely because of that. All that you know, whether about social relationships, buying stuff or your work, you weren't born with any of that knowledge. You came here like a blank slate as the behaviourists would tell you. Your mind was empty and you knew nothing till you were taught and therefore learned.

You learned from other people and today you have an opinion on literally everything because you've observed others, whether friends or family, strangers or even the role models you've never met. It took a variety of people for you to be where you are or where you're going. Remember the school teachers that invested in you and taught you beyond the curriculum. Not forgetting who paid your fees and made sure you had all the resources you needed at school.

Remember those bursaries and loans before you start saying that qualification is all because of you. No matter how deserving you think you were, the fact is, you wouldn't have it if not for those institutions that make it possible for people to further their studies even though they cannot afford it. In addition, remember all the places you went to even though your family could not afford to take you, the activities you participated in, leadership roles and many other opportunities given to you.

Despite your powerful brain, mind, personality and character, all these little things played a major role in your life. Opportunities were presented to you and that's why you should give others the same and even more opportunities when you can. Someone gave you an opportunity and that's why you must also do the same. Just because things were tough for you doesn't mean you should make it tough for everyone else.

It's bad enough that you suffered, stop carrying all that suffering into other people's lives when you can help. If you can make someone else's journey a little easier and a little bit more bearable, if you can help, if there's anything at all that you can do, no matter how small, kindly just do it. If you can afford to buy one child who's not yours Christmas clothing or even pay just one student's fees. It all counts no matter how small it is.

Give other people a chance, believe in others and help them with the resources they need to get to where you are. We really need to start building a world where success is not exclusive. Not just for me and you but those around us too. Do things to benefit others. Open doors for people who've lived their entire lives behind closed doors. If you can, just do it. Not tomorrow, not next month or as a 2014 resolution, just do it today, do it now in fact.

It's really saddening how once people make it, they build a hedge and it's almost like they live in their own little castles or paradise. Just because life is nice and easy and you don't struggle to get what you want doesn't mean millions of other people aren't struggling out there. We really need to stop living like celebrities who have no family name and families that are neither known nor heard of. You have a family, you have a community or an institution that brought you up, well unless you're Tarzan!

So never forget where you come from and who was there for you. Never forget who recognised you, granted you that opportunity and those who gave you exactly what you needed when no-one else could. Never forget those people. Be like little children, they are helpless and know they cannot survive on their own.

Likewise, we would not have been where we are on our own. Stop saying you made it all by yourself because alone you couldn't have. Acknowledge those who helped and contributed to making you the intelligent, smart and strong person you are today because you are not self-made!

PRICE FOLLOWS EARNINGS

Over the long term, the single most fundamental driver of price is earnings and only earnings (Franco Busetti). Therefore, share price always follows earnings in the long run. This means that if a company keeps delivering great earnings/profits, it's only a matter of time before their share price improves. As human beings we have our own personal 'share price' which is how much we earn. If we continue to bring value into an organisation/institution, our own personal share price (salaries) will eventually have no choice but to improve.

I don't know when last you applied for a job or had an interview but I know things have changed a lot in whom and how companies employ. Large companies are very exclusive when seeking to employ people. They have multiple steps before you even get to the interview and many never make it to that stage. Online assessments, written and oral tests, presentations and many other things are done before one gets to the interview or even after the interview. And there are even more interviews after the first.

These processes are extensive, intensive and quite demanding. For the candidates, they might seem unnecessary and just too much work. Ironically, these companies often seek new employees yet disqualify many applicants. You may be wondering why. I think it's most probably because they understand that price follows earnings. You see in the end, every company is a business and profit is key. For very company to achieve their business goals, particularly earnings or profit depends largely on the employees.

That's why companies take great caution as to whom they employ. Every company wants someone who will bring value to their organisation. They are looking for innovative and creative people who think out of the box, people who will come up with new and practical ideas and strategies to achieve the significant business goals. Every company wants to grow bigger and better in themselves and over their competitors, and that's why it's important to employ people who will bring value to them and work towards these goals.

Not everyone can do that, in fact very few people can do that and thus not just anyone gets employed no matter how qualified or even over-qualified they are. It's all about value and if you can't prove to them that value is what you have then you're not a suitable candidate. Companies are looking for people who will bring them value so before you apply for that job, ask yourself if you'll bring value to them. This is what you really need to ask yourself even when you go for interviews because they sure will ask you.

I guess another reason these companies got smart is because people claim a lot these days. They claim to be what they're not 'the best money can buy' 'the best in the industry' 'a loss to those who don't employ them.' We live in a generation where people master the art of self-branding. They know how to sell and market themselves. These people can sell sushi to an 80 year old Zulu man from rural KZN. That's just how great they are yet cannot do what they promise to. They do not fulfil what they offer to bring. All talk and no action.

The point is this, companies and even people, are willing to pay a premium for value. All you really need to increase your share price or income is to increase the value you bring. Are you a valuable member to your company or a waste of the company's resources? Bring value and you won't have to be the second option!

FINDING A GOOD MENTOR IS LIKE FINDING A GREAT INVESTMENT ADVISER

We all want the best investment advisers and mentors we can get. With investors in particular, we want the best money can buy because their advice has major implications. In most cases though, the best investment advisors and mentors usually have many clients or mentees. So if you want a busy person to be your mentor, you must be able to answer a few questions including the following:

Ø Why do you need a mentor?
Ø Where are you headed to and how can a mentor assist you?
Ø Why this particular mentor?
Ø Why should this mentor invest his or her time on you?

You can't go request a mentor when you have no clue where you're headed. This is what happened when I approached Billy Selekane CSP (Certified Speaking Professional) to mentor me. He asked me a lot of questions and if I didn't know what I wanted, I would have given up and said 'he doesn't want to mentor me.'

So before you go with the recent mentor trend, be sure you know what it takes. It's a sacrifice to mentor someone and it may be a fashionable thing these days but it's actually quite serious. You must have a very clear and not vague idea about where you're going. In addition, mentors are not there to spoon-feed you or make decisions for you. They do not choose your path but only give the necessary guidance, knowledge and wisdom so don't expect your mentor to be your brain.

Same goes for investment advisers, their duty is to advice. They may give you all the information you need and tell you all the possible outcomes but they'll never make the decision for you. In the end, the decision lies with you. The choice is always yours. Remember it's your life, your choices and consequences to bear not theirs. So don't give others a responsibility they already have with their own lives.

ALL TRENDS EVENTUALLY END

This is a very powerful thing because even when I observed the financial markets, I realised that just as much as no economic boom lasts forever, there's also no economic contraction that lasts forever. So indeed, good or bad, nothing lasts forever. If you are going through your own "personal recession" where everything is not working, please be comforted; this too shall pass.

Good or bad, all trends eventually end. There will always be new highs and new lows. What was low once may suddenly be high and likewise, what was once high may unexpectedly be low. It's a basic human condition, good or bad, change will always happen. It's inevitable. So if you're having a difficult time, I repeat, take comfort in knowing that this too shall pass because nothing lasts forever.

Let's get a bit political now. The apartheid era started in 1948 and only ended in 1994. Take into consideration that the racial segregation had already started before the apartheid government came into power. We all know how tough this era was for most South Africans especially the black population. At that time, people must have had very little hope, particularly in the 1940s and 50s (early years). They however had to endure and survive, they had to adapt and make a living under such conditions. It might have looked like it will never end but people fought and it eventually did.

Women are another group that has been oppressed for many years but kept fighting for gender equality and recognition. It might not be perfect, but women are now more valued and honoured in society than they were in the 1960s. Their voices matter now and they are much more respected and seen as legitimate authority than they were 30 years ago. During the intense struggle, this may have appeared to be an unrealistic dream or fantasy but some women saw the hope and kept fighting, and now woman's social standing has improved in society.

The key point is this, nothing lasts forever, and it all comes to an end. So when times get tough, you have to keep fighting because no matter how further down in the ladder you are, there's always hope. No matter how dark the past was, the present may be the greatest and no matter how difficult the present is, the future will be better.

And I'm not talking future as in months or years because I know people have a tendency to postpone their present happiness for the future. For example, people wait for Friday to be happy and spend the whole week in misery and some say they can't be content until they get a car. The reality is, you can still be happy and content even without it because you may eventually get it and still be unhappy for some reason or another.

So this is not the tomorrow I was referring to here. I'm talking about a better tomorrow even though today has been a nightmare (as in right now on this very day). The Joburg weather is a perfect example in this instance. This is by far the most unstable thing I know. It can be very cold, dark and rainy today and you wake up to the brightest, shining and hot sun tomorrow morning. People in Cape Town might disagree. Anyway, consider the quote below:

"If you are in a bad situation, don't worry, it will change. If you are in a good situation, don't worry it will change."
John A Simon Sr.

I think most of us have heard that before and this is why the above quote is significant. It reminds us that we can never think only bad things come to an end because so does the great and even best things in life. This is why you can never think you got it, you can never be too comfortable and think you are there and nothing can touch you because it will.

Even in the most perfect conditions, storms hit. I'm sure you've seen it yourself. You wake up to a bright shiny day, put on something light and regret it after 2 hours when the weather starts changing. Out of nowhere it gets dark, cold and starts pouring. And there you were thinking, 'what a beautiful weather it is, I can even go for a picnic.'

In reality then, we cannot afford to be complacent because something might just go wrong. I'm not saying you must be weary and constantly worried that something bad will happen. I'm neither saying you should ruin a great moment by saying things like 'every time something good happens to me, I know it won't last or something bad is about to happen.' No, that's not the way to go.

You should actually enjoy and in fact, indulge and savour every great moment without thinking such things. An important issue that comes up here is the psychological concept of mindfulness. This basically means living in the now and being aware of the present conditions and making most of them. However in so doing, kindly be aware that things will not always be rosy. This is planet earth, not a fantasy land. Bad things happen to good people and even in the perfect time when we think nothing can ruin this. Life happens and it always will.

What I want to encourage here is that even though good and bad both come to an end, you shouldn't be waiting for conditions to be perfect for you to accomplish something. You cannot say, 'oh I'm waiting for this bad season to pass so my life can go on' or 'sadly when this awesome vacation ends, I'm going back to my normal boring life.' You should instead choose to enjoy the good times and endure the hard times alike, knowing that none are permanent and both will pass.

OVERCONFIDENCE IS AS BAD AS LACK OF CONFIDENCE

In the financial markets, just like in life, lack of overconfidence is as bad as lack of confidence. Some people have a lack of confidence and others have too much of it and both extremes are not healthy. When you're overconfident, no one can teach you anything because 'you got this,' you don't need anybody because you have it all under control.

In the financial markets, when people become overconfident, they stop doing the things that they used to do. Maybe they used to conduct a fundamental analysis to understand the intrinsic value of a share but now all they do is speculate and base their investments strategies on assumptions and unfounded predictions.

Never be overconfident, my friend. Keep calm and do what you've always been doing. If you're now in a position of authority, it doesn't mean you've made it. Keep investing in yourself, attend leadership seminars, you can just never know enough. There's always something new to hear, see and learn. Open your eyes, ears and mind and stop feeling too big for your shoes.

The key here is to avoid both extremes. It's really sad to see people with talent lacking confidence. This lack of confidence seems to be more prevalent in black communities because even parents pull their own children down by the manner in which they address them. For example, parents who call their kids a 'dom kop.'

Perhaps the really sad thing here is that even the parents don't see what this does to their children. Children internalise these names and it gets difficult to break out of such chains particularly because even your parents play a major role in it. As a result, these children have a low self-esteem and get easily embarrassed. They tend to be scared of complaining and put themselves down. They believe others deserve to shine and not them. They therefore feel unworthy and lack confidence and assertiveness.

It's really funny to see how this lack of confidence plays out, especially in restaurants. When a white person wants to get a take-away, they will confidently ask and expect the waiters to do that immediately whereas the black person will firstly be hesitant to raise their hand and when they eventually do, they shamefully and apologetically ask the waiters as if they aren't paying for that service.

I've never seen so much confidence as that possessed by Indian people. One of my Indian neighbours came to my house once and confidently instructed me to give him ice because he had many visitors and was out of ice. Note that I said confidently, not shy, looking down and begging. You've got to love the confidence that Indian people have. The black nation sure needs a bit of that spice.

In conclusion, the key principle here is that of moderation. Even philosophers will tell you my friend, there should neither excess nor deficiency is good for your health, everything should just be in the correct balance. And as the common saying goes, 'too much of anything is not good.' Likewise, it's important to moderate our confidence levels and have neither too much nor too little but just enough or the necessary level we need depending on the situation.

PEOPLE JUDGE YOU HARSHLY WHEN YOU'RE UNTESTED, IT'S NOT PERSONAL: FOCUS ON THE WORK AND THEY'LL COME AROUND

When former President Thabo Mbeki was inaugurated as president in 1999, the rand fell to more than R6.00 to the dollar for the first time. The rand fell even further when Tito Mboweni was appointed Governor of the South African Reserve Bank. Isn't it interesting that the same people who were nervous when Mbeki was elected president and Mboweni appointed governor are now praising both men for fiscal discipline? Those who were nervous are now their biggest fans.

This is the same thing that will happen to you when you get a new role. People will get nervous, they will criticize you and some won't even give you the support you deserve. This has very little to do with you as a person so don't take it personal. There's really no need to see it as a personal attack so rather see it as normal. I'm sure you've been a participant in this yourself.

Remember when you got a new boss, a new roommate or a new lecture in the second term? Admit it, it was a bit uncomfortable at first, you compared them to the old ones and discredited them based on this comparison.

This appears to be another one of those human conditions. We're just more comfortable with the old and change seems to be unsettling at first. That's why people ought to be given a chance. Do not immediately disqualify any-one because they're not like your old boss. Just because they do certain things differently doesn't mean they're doing it wrong. Think about it, if they were your first boss, you wouldn't have had much of a problem with their way of doing things. You would've adapted instead.

So my friends, when you get that first job, relax and be yourself. Adapt to your new environment and people. When you slip up and get scolded in front of everyone, when your boss humiliates you and your colleagues don't seem to like you, remember why you're there and just do your job. Focus on your work and do it with utmost competence. Be a diligent worker and a loyal employee, it always pay off.

Likewise, if you get into a new role or position and people find it a bit hard to warm up to you, be patient. Don't take it to head and don't push yourself too hard. You really don't need to devote much effort to try winning their approval or buying their kindness. And sometimes people genuinely won't click with you and you won't click with them, it's not personal, it's just a part of life. You won't like everyone you meet and neither will you be liked by everyone who meets you. Accept this and move over on.

In all these circumstances though, just be yourself and do your best. Keep quiet, work hard and you will see your critics turn into fans. So focus on the work and be the professional that you are. You're not there for personal vendettas in any case!

YOU CANNOT JUDGE SOMEONE'S POTENTIAL BY THEIR PAST. GIVE PEOPLE A CHANCE!

In the financial markets: "100% of the information you have about a company represents the past, and yet 100% of the value depends on the future." Bill Miller

Sometimes we focus too much on the past than we ought to. I'm not trying to disqualify nor discredit the impact of the past on the present nor future. It's only that we sometimes give the past much more power than it deserves. I'm quite certain that if the past could talk directly to us, it would tell each and every one of us to just leave it alone and live in the present. The problem appears to be our tendency to drag things along instead of letting go. In short, "sithand' umthwalo" meaning, we like carrying heavy burdens.

It's truly sad how the past dominates the present and influences our future expectations. The past is now like MTN, everywhere you go. Today I want you to ask yourself this: How much of this past are you willing to leave behind? How long will you keep dragging the past you haven't left behind? I really don't get why we can't seem to grasp the meaning of 'past.' The past is exactly that, the past!

It is history, it is gone and you can't change it so stop re-living and living in it. If you really want the past to leave you alone, guess what, it doesn't. You leave it alone. You choose to leave it behind. It's as much of a choice as you choosing to read this book now. You choose how much of the past will affect your present and future. You choose to ensure that the past stays where it belongs, in the past.

This doesn't mean we simply float through life pretending it didn't happen. We don't ignore it, we learn from it instead and you'll hear more about this in the next chapter. The point here is that we all have a past: good, bad, perfect or shady, we all have it and none of us can intentionally clear it, it's unfortunately cleared only through psychological disorders like Dementia. In general, we all can't clear it, there's just no delete button.

Perhaps the key issue here is why we can't accept the past as it is and move over it. Just do yourself a favour and stop trying to alter it, stop wishing what you could have or shouldn't have done, what should have or not have happened. None of this will change a thing; it won't change anything at all.

The sooner we accept our past the least surprised we'll also be about other people's past. We'll be more open-minded and learn that we all lived before we got to where we are now. We made some serious mistakes, blunders and huge flops. We don't have to hide it, we don't have to run from it and absolutely don't need to lie about it. The more you do any of these things, the more control you give your past over your present and future.

Accept your humanity, set yourself free by accepting that it all happened and there's absolutely nothing you can do about it. Stop using it against yourself and stop using other people's past against them as well. Like I said, if you admit and accept yours, you'll be more sensitive and understanding towards other's past.

I'm clearly proposing the Golden Rule here: do unto others as you'd like them to do unto you. Would you like it if people continuously rubbed your past on your face? Would you like it if you didn't get that job or promotion because of some silly thing you did in the past? Of course not so don't do it to others too!

You can't move forward with you back faced forward, only with your head in that direction. Your eyes must look forward and your back must stay at the back for you to move forward. Likewise, stop pointing people back to their past. Choose to move forward and stop looking back.

Stop allowing the past to interfere with how you evaluate people or circumstances. Don't evaluate nor discredit people based on their past because I'm sure there's a lot in your past that would've discredited you and disqualified you from being where you are now! Choose to look and live in the present. Don't dismiss anyone because of their past failures because yours would surely dismiss you too. You got a second chance so kindly give it to others.

Leave other people's past in the past and see their current potential. If the financial markets depended on the past, it would've long ceased to exist. Learn from this that fluctuations are inevitable and as mentioned earlier, past performance does not predict future performance. People who've made unwise choices in the past can make wise choices today and even better choices in future.

Contrary to popular belief, a leopard does change its spots. Yes, they may vaguely be there because the past can never be completely removed but a turn-around is always possible. Look at yourself as an example, be it from past failed relationships, how you used to waste money or was always in debt, how you used to be lazy or a procrastinator yet today none of these things can be used to describe you because it's just not who you are anymore.

This is because there's always a second chance. An opportunity to make things right always awaits and you choose to grab it with both hands or let it slip through your fingers. I'm sure you grabbed it so have some bit of faith, if you could do it, so could they.

This reminds me of Steve Jobs, the CEO and co-founder of Apple who lost the company's board members trust in 1985 and was expelled. Sales dropped drastically during the period of his dismissal and several years later, he went back to Apple and played a major role in revolutionizing the digital music and mobile phone industry. We all know how great Apple is today, you probably have or want an i-everything (laptop, phone, tab). What's worth wondering here is where the company would've been had Jobs not been given a second chance and returned.

So fortunately for us, we live in a world of loosers and I'm not calling Jobs a looser nor talking about the biggest looser competition. All I'm saying is, we live in a world where people and companies that failed big time have managed to bounce back. So today, be the person who helps others get back up when they've been knocked down, not the one who further puts them down and leaves them helpless.

See the potential in others, it may be just what they need. You may just be their only hope so give them a hand, help them get back up, give them a kick in the right direction. Sometimes all people really need is that one person who'll see potential in them despite their past. The person who will tell them 'I believe in you, don't give up, you have a great potential.' Why won't you be that person today?

I once saw someone wearing a t-shirt written "every saint has a past, every sinner has a future." You may be high and mighty right now but you know you didn't get there without several or rather numerous falls and errors. Give others a chance just as you've been given new beginnings and a fresh start. There's always potential light in every dark past and besides, people without a dark past (if they exist) aren't necessarily saints either.

Not everyone who comes into your life with impact will have a clean background, unless they washed and covered it super clean with Mr Muscles. I'm just saying that you must expect perfection from no-one because past failures and blunders are inevitable. Remember where you yourself come from!

So before you tell someone they won't amount to anything, before you tell someone they aren't going to make it because of their past, think of all the people who made it through the hardships. Think of all the great musicians who were told they couldn't sing to save their lives, the actors who were rejected multiple times because they just weren't good enough. In sum: CAUTION: Don't judge someone's potential based on their past. Give people a chance!

ON THE OTHER HAND A LESSON FROM THE ECONOMISTS

Economists love using the phrase "on the other hand" and one day in 2007 when my business was not doing well at all, I thought of this phrase differently. Business was really bad during that period. I had been adversely listed in credit bureaus, sued by one of the companies we owed money, my car was repossessed and I was approaching depression.

On the other hand though, I was in my first year as an MBA student, I had just married the most beautiful and wise woman, Thabang. Spiritually, I was stronger than ever and I was still alive and healthy. It hit me that I was not counting my blessings and I realised how ungrateful I had become. I know I'm not the only one guilty of this.

Isn't it ironic how when some things, even if it's just one little thing not going well, we have a tendency to live as if nothing's going right? I guess it's because different parts of our lives are like a body, very much interconnected. When one part of the body is sick, it affects the whole body and thus feels as though the whole body is sick. Our emotions and thoughts also get sick somehow. I guess that's why when things aren't going well only in business, relationship or family, it gets a bit more difficult to look at the many other things going right.

This process may seem natural and is thus a mission to overcome but in general, to conquer it requires that we consciously cultivate an attitude of gratitude. Look at the stars, when it's dark and rainy, most of them become invisible and hardly shine, but there are always those few stars that come out if you look closely. There's always that one bright star. We should view our lives in the same manner by learning to consciously look for that bright star in dark and troubled times.

We must look for the things that are going well. As long as you're alive, you can never run out of reasons to be thankful. The very fact that you woke up and are breathing is enough to get you thankful. However, because we always want this and that, we always want things to go like this and not like that, we are more susceptible to complaining, grumbling and getting upset over things going the way they shouldn't be.

I know things might be hard for you, maybe you've been divorced, lost a loved one or even got retrenched. I know it's not as easy as it sounds but before you wallop in self-pity, please do me a favour, kindly pause and think about the things 'on the other hand.' Is there really nothing to be grateful for? Nothing at all..?

You work as a cashier and still complain about your job, think about the guy who's been looking for a job for over 5 years now and is still unemployed. Better yet, think about the times when you were unemployed.

And if you have a terminal illness and have given up all hope even though the doctors say you can still live a few more years, before you complain, think about the person who died of an acute illness simply because they did not have medical aid, proper hygiene, sanitation or nutrition.

Learn to look on the other hand like the economists, appreciate the little things and see the light at the end of the tunnel because it's always there no matter how small it is. A candle light in the biggest and darkest hall still shines, so when the left hand is cold and dark, look beyond it to see the light and sun in the right. Appreciate the small things that go right. There's always a reason to smile, laugh and be happy. If you look for it, you will find it!

THERE IS SOMETHING CALLED TOO MUCH DIVERSIFICATION – THOSE WHO GET TO THE TOP ARE FOCUSSED AND SINGLE-MINDED

In the financial markets, diversification occurs when people invest in various assets because they want to reduce their overall risk. In such cases, they have multiple investments including stocks, real estate or mutual funds. The aim here is to diversify and avoid putting too much into one investment. The ultimate goal in the financial markets, particularly in investments is to avoid putting all your eggs in one basket because it's risky. If one egg breaks the entire basket gets contaminated and nobody wants that, which makes perfect sense.

Likewise, there's absolutely nothing wrong with diversifying, expanding your horizons and being an overall involved person. I'm a good example here. As seen in about the author, I'm a professional speaker, MC and Chairman among other things. The reality is, no matter how much you diversify so in general, diversification is a great thing. However, your risk is never entirely eliminated and that's why you must always choose to diversify wisely. As Warren Buffett said, "Wide diversification is only required when investors do not understand what they are doing."

People who know and understand what they're doing don't need too much diversification indeed. As I stated earlier, people who get to the top are those that are focused and single-minded. In order to invest in yourself and get much out of it, you ought to choose what deserves most of your focus. You can't necessarily operate on the markets phenomena here. You can't put in 20% to your permanent job, 30% to your part-time job, 30% to your own business, 10% on the family business and the other 10% on your friend's business.

Talk about mission impossible. The reality is, you can't do too many things at once and thus it's important to strike a balance rather than create the false sense of security that comes with too much diversification.

It's absolutely impossible to strike a balance when you don't have a clear, straightforward and important goal that deserves most of your focus. You must therefore choose the goal you're willing to strive for and devote most of your time and energy to. Think about it, how many successful people who've made it so to speak, were involved in too many things? When you Google a person considered to be successful in the music industry, what comes up first? It's definitely not their advertising career.

In the end, what you invest more in, what you devote yourself more to will outlast everything else. So today, choose to clarify your goals and stop trying this and that, chasing the wind blowing to the east then to the west and back to the east. If this is how you do things, trust me when I say you won't get too far in anything unless there is some form of correlation.

Therefore, in order to handle diversification wisely, at least correlate your diverse activities, it makes things easier to handle and manage. For example, it's easier for celebrities to be an actor, singer and host at the same time than to be an electrical engineer and a singer. There must be coherence in your diversification to avoid wearing yourself out and losing yourself in your diverse activities. Avoid confusion, too much work and exhaustion by clearly defining your goals and passion so you can invest in them more.

You can't loose focus on what you do best by doing too many things at once. You can't allow yourself to get involved in things because your friend got into business and it worked out for him. Stop competing with others because it'll awfully wear you out. Accept that different things work for different people and that you can't do everything you wish to do or try out everything you think you can do. Some things are not for you to do, some things are better done by others than you. That's why choice is vital here. You must choose what's worthwhile for you.

In addition, sometimes you must admit when you've been defeated and stop forcing or chasing things that aren't there. Sometimes a loss is a loss and it costs more to fix than to quit it. If for example you made a huge investment and things didn't turn out as you hoped and you incurred a huge loss and debt instead, you can't try to fix it when absolutely nothing can be done. It will only hurt your pocket even more if you try to make it work so sometimes it's better to close a door and let another open.

Therefore, examine what's working and what isn't. If the investment you made is not yielding substantial returns, change your direction, strategy and plan. As you can see here, sometimes diversification is unnecessary. Be wise and have valid reasons that won't hurt you, your pocket or health. When you have too many things going on, it might be good to know you're doing something but all that may not be very beneficial because they all have a small portion of your focus.

You can't focus on things that give you little return. Just like in the markets, successful businesses never compromise core business goals and operations for peripheral ones. You must always focus on the core dimensions of whatever you do because it your focus is diversified and nothing gets the best of you, nothing will yield the results that come with devotion to clear goals and passions. Therefore, choose focus and single-mindedness to get to the top.

 BULL MARKETS ALWAYS LAST LONGER THAN BEAR MARKETS – BE BULLISH

"Since 1961, the average bull market has lasted 65 months while the average bear market has only lasted 17 months." Franco Busetti. Tough times never last! The good and high times (bull markets) always last longer than the bad and low times (bear markets). So if things aren't going well today, be comforted. Be bullish my friend, expect things to go well in your life. Expect that job, that increase, that husband, expect it to come rushing to you – be bullish.

As you learned about the significance of vigilance in the earlier chapters, I would like to think that you are now vigilant because if you don't keep watch, the bull may turn around to injure you no matter how young, old, experienced or inexperienced you are. Change is inevitable in the markets. This is why it's significant to be vigilant even though you've been in business for a very long time and you know and understand all there is to it. Always keep watch my friend because the season may change from bull domination to bear supremacy in an instant.

Bulls are bulls because they are larger than the female cows and are capable of fighting and winning over a bear. They are stronger and tougher. They possess features assisting in domination and superiority and can surely put up a fight and win.

Even in the animal kingdom, the bull's lifespan is longer than the bear's. Whereas the bear lives for around 20 years, the bull's lifespan is 20-25 years and thus usually 5 years longer than the bear's. Moreover, bears are more vulnerable to extinction than bulls and even sleep for over 3 months during winter. Bulls on the other hand are least threatened to become extinct and they never sleep that long. Therefore even when there seems to be no light at the moment and it appears as though your good times are sleeping, remember that it's never for long.

The truth is, no matter what you're going through now, nothing lasts forever. You may be crying now but you won't always be in tears. Unfortunately for us we cannot be like bears and sleep in winter. We should actually be thankful that life doesn't even come with that option. You cannot sleep for the two most difficult weeks of your life and wake up when it's all over. You must bear it, endure it and let it build you. It will bring out something in you, whether the best or worst is up to you.

The strength and courage of a bear is what we need to survive the bear markets so when times get rough, be strengthened and courageous. Use your own postures and strategies to survive. Bears are typically solitary animals and represent the opposite of bulls. You'll often realise that you're alone in tough times and that's why it's important to build your own personal resources.

It is indeed true that tough times never last but tough people do. That's why even in bull-fighting, not just any bull can participate. Only certain bulls, with a certain length, weight and years can participate. Therefore merely being human doesn't mean you can fight, survive and succeed. It means we all have the potential but only certain people can fight and overcome the tough times with victory.

Tough people survive, they keep their hope and optimism even when the situation seems impossible. They keep holding on no matter how hopeless it seems. They believe in miracles and always expect the best even though circumstances don't allow them to. Tough people persevere and never give up. They can put up a fight like bulls and actually win over the bears.

 # PAST PERFORMANCE IS NO GUARANTEE FOR FUTURE RESULTS

"It is wise to keep in mind that neither success nor failure is ever final." Roger Babson

I want to focus on the former part of this quote, "It is wise to keep in mind that success is not final." One can gather from this quote that a victory does not necessarily put a full stop. One victory doesn't end the story, its one incident, and only one chapter of a book. The story goes on even after your major success so never be too comfortable and rest on your past victory or success.

We see it in the financial markets, a company might be doing very well and all of a sudden boom, it goes down just like that. So just because you've been doing well doesn't guarantee that you'll do well in future. Let's take it to the grassroots, remember when you were a varsity student and some students had passed the commercial subjects brilliantly in high school yet dismally failed a BCom Accounting or Finance in varsity? Additionally, some got very high semester marks and exam entry yet a very low exam mark, and for others, the exact opposite happened.

Here's the point, human beings have a tendency to think just because they've made it, they will always make it. We somehow tend to think that the past determines the future and in some instances it does but this is not always the case, especially with regards to success. The truth is, sometimes you won't do well even though you've done really well in the past.

Remember how Nokia was a very well-known and most recommended cell-phone company 10 years ago? Well, it's not so much today. Nokia had the largest market share then and they somehow got overtaken by many other cell-phone companies like Samsung and Apple. You can be the best at some point and may not necessarily stay there. In America, half of the current 500 top Standard and Poor's (S&Ps) companies by market capitalisation were not there 50 years ago.

Some of the companies that were there years back are non-existent today and some just got overtaken by others.

The fact is, when you do well and start slacking, someone will overtake you. The biggest mistake you can make is thinking that you've made it and start relaxing. Take South Africa for example: In 2013, we've been overtaken by Mauritius in both the World Bank Ease of doing business report as well as the World Economic Forum's Global Competitive Index.

In sub-Saharan Africa, we have always been on top but our position is not guaranteed anymore. In the October 2012 Economist magazine, I read that Nigeria which has been a distant second in terms of the size of their economy as measured by the Gross Domestic Product (GDP), may in fact overtake South Africa in the next decade or two. This in fact might even be earlier as mentioned in the Forbes Africa publication in September 2013 because Nigeria is busy with a re-base of their economy.

So don't make the common mistake of fighting to be the best and relaxing once we do because we think we'll always be there. Complacency is not an option. Don't just fight to get there, fight to stay on top. You must preserve your position or else you will loose it. You may not always have that job. If someone else does better than you, you will be overtaken and get left behind. Never deceive yourself into thinking that you're irreplaceable because trust me, you are.

Look at yourself and those around you, it's very rare to find a person in the same position they were in 20 years ago. Over a long period, you get promoted, demoted or even fired. As the CEO of your life, you also decide who gets which position. Think about the people in your social network, and I mean your real network of friends not your 10 000 Twitter followers or 2000 Facebook friends.

The reality is, someone who was your closest friend 10 years ago may be like a stranger to you now because people come and go like soapie characters in our lives. Some are given a bigger role, others get fewer parts and others exit the show altogether. Just because one was once the star of the show doesn't mean they'll always be.

The point is, if someone in that friendship becomes distant and now has less time for you than they did, you'll disconnect and won't stay closest friend for long if that goes on long enough. Consider also some of the people you've known for over 10 years yet are still just acquaintances. What does this tell you? People determine their position in your life and so do you in theirs. Same with your job, you determine how long you will stay and where you will stay.

So, keep doing what you did to get there. If you worked hard, committed and devoted yourself to it, keep that energy, keep that drive and motivation. Another way of looking at this is that even though you didn't do well in the past, you can be elevated and end up doing very well.

Back to the soapie, just as much as the star may not shine anymore, so can the characters move from appearing once a week to becoming the main character and even the star of the show. This further teaches us how we must never overlook or underestimate the significance of small beginnings because starting small doesn't mean you'll always be small. All this proves to us that how you've performed in the past does not guarantee your future performance.

HUMILIATION IS A PART OF LIFE, DEAL WITH IT

In my view, no-one can teach us how to deal with humiliation better than our president, he just moves on. You most probably remember the painting saga. The latest is also seen in the recent World Economic Forum (WEF). President Jacob Zuma went to the WEF in Davos intending to reassure the world that South Africa welcomed mining investors. A few days before, Mineral Resources Minister Susan Shabangu launched a broadside of remarkable ferocity and insensitivity against Anglo American and its subsidiary, Anglo American Platinum (Amplats).

The two culprits had had the nerve to announce their business proposals without talking to her. In addition to this, there was more provocation from the ANC Secretary-General Gwede Mantashe. On the SABC radio debate, he offered this conciliatory thought to "welcome investor" Anglo: "You come in here and steal our money and treat us like visitors, like second-class citizens... you treat us with utter disdain, Shane Mark Cutifani, welcome to the top job at Anglo American!" How embarrassing does it get for Mr President? One can only imagine.

The reality is that people get humiliated all the time. It's just a part of life and you're not an exception. Whether it was undeserved, unfair or embarrassing is not the point, the point is how you handle it. It's really inevitable so because preparation always guarantees success, you must make up your mind from before you actually get humiliated that you will not let it keep you down but dare to move on.

Sometimes we do a good job of humiliating ourselves and feel stupid about it later and we feel like we can't face people or even the world for that matter. Well when this happens, honestly, just dust yourself off and get back up. Keep walking like Johnny Walker. Yes, it is that simple, no matter how huge the embarrassment. If you keep hiding, you're just making life difficult for yourself so that really doesn't help. Also, if you keep dwelling on it you give people power to use it against you. You must decide within yourself that yes it happened but no, I won't let it do any more damage to me or my life than it already has.

It's really okay to feel embarrassed about whatever that humiliated you but don't dwell there for too long. So what if you made a really bad investment choice and you feel stupid because of all the losses incurred? So what if people talk to you like that or tell others about the most embarrassing thing that ever happened to you? If they're laughing about it, join the club and stop tearing! They won't move on unless you do so show them you don't care and neither will they!

And if your boss literally screams at you in front of everyone, you can't afford to cry like a sissy in the office, you have got to find a better way of coping. Not through retaliation of course, but accept that it happened and stop reminiscing about it over and over because it will only do more damage than good. Humiliation works because we take things too seriously sometimes. Learn to laugh at yourself and get back up.

It's quite ironic how we often claim 'I don't care what they say or think about me' yet what really gets to us when we feel humiliated is the anxiety that comes with knowing others saw or heard that. Imagine how many CEO's, companies, celebrities and other people or institutions would have had their careers, jobs and businesses lost if they took every stride of humiliation to head.

Imagine if every form of humiliation kept them down because they took it personally. I'm certain that if this were the case, most people would not be where they are. So through all your humiliation, no matter how huge, sad and indenting it is, rise up and move on. People have survived the worst and besides, it's got to take more than that to bring and keep you down!

IF YOUR FRIEND EVER ASKS YOU WHO ROBERT MUGAB IS, TERMINATE THAT FRIENDSHIP!

Honestly though, imagine someone you confidently refer to as your friend asking you this. That is just a major friendship offense right there. It really does matter who your friends are and what you guys do and say to each other. You may not realize it but these are some of the most influential people in your life. They are pretty much like a broker, the person that helps you make some major financial decisions.

These are the people you go to when you need some real advice and input that will have a major influence in your life. They play a very valuable role in your life and that's why it's important to select them carefully. You don't just take a person with a rough idea about the financial markets to be your broker. You need a well-informed and qualified person.

We most probably don't have a friendship scale to measure how qualified people are to be our friends but you nonetheless need to take caution with whom you choose to be friends with, whom you spend your time with and the influence they have in your life. The fact is, whoever you spend your time with most, whoever you listen to most rubs off on you and they significantly influence your perceptions, beliefs and choices.

I read a study once and I unfortunately can't remember where I read it but I won't forget the results because they were very eye-opening. In this study, it was found that a person will be as successful as the average of the five people closest to him or her. So that's why it's important whom you let into your inner circle. If your friends don't challenge and motivate you to be a better person, if your friends ask you who Mugabe is, you can clearly see where your success is.

Another significant thing one needs to understand about friendship is that people come and go in our lives. Some friendships are permanent and long-term and some are temporary and seasonal. You cannot keep holding on to winter clothes in this hot weather, you cannot wear the clothes you wore when you were a size 30 because you're now a 36. They won't fit because you're a bigger size now and the really warm winter clothes are irrelevant in a hot summer season. They serve no purpose.

Likewise, some friends really aren't meant to be in your life any longer than they have. When the season is gone, accept and let go. Get over it. It served the purpose and it's over now. Appreciate the moments, impact and memories but do not hold on to them. When the time is gone, it is gone, you can't keep pushing and forcing to make it work when it really can't or won't.

If your broker no longer serves you, gives you the correct or relevant information and leads you to making poor decisions then you really have to let them go. If their input is no longer valuable and they add nothing of value to your decisions, then they no longer have a role. You cannot keep dragging people who are pulling you down and serve no purpose in your life. Likewise, let go of all the friendships that were once great yet are doing you no good right now. It doesn't make them bad people, it's just how life goes.

Sometimes people aren't where you are anymore. Maybe you disconnected or you now see, believe and enjoy different things. Your future or paths are now headed in opposite directions and you no longer have any positive impact on each other. Stop wasting each other's time and move on already! People and things are very dynamic and change is inevitable. When things have changed for the worst and friendship is no longer enjoyable and impactful then it's time to exit!

IN THE FINANCIAL MARKETS, JUST LIKE IN LIFE: NOBODY CARES HOW GOOD YOU USED TO BE

Chief Executives will know this: Shareholders are ruthless – the fact that you have given them solid performance in the past 10 years, means absolutely nothing to them. If they start suspecting that the prospects of your company are not that great, they will sell their shares and move on. They don't care how good you used to be. This is also true about life; we simply don't care how good you used to be.

We really don't care about the amazing thing you did back in 1981. A good example here is our national football team Bafana Bafana. The team was once on top of their game and the best in Africa, but now they hardly qualify in the African Cup of Nations and they still celebrate even though they didn't qualify. It has almost become normal for them to not qualify. What we see and think about them today is solely based on their current performance and not their past victories.

The fact is if you're still celebrating the achievement you got over 10 years ago, get over it. Nobody cares what you were 10 years ago, it's about what you are today. Bafana Bafana is not the best in Africa today, it was then and they can't be celebrating their 1996 victory in 2013. It's about their recent wins and losses. So congrats if you achieved something huge in 1981 but what are you doing at this very moment.

Are your skills current? Are you still doing the things you were doing then? If you aren't, then we really don't care what you were doing many moons ago when we weren't even born! It's really about the now and what you're doing now is what matters.

If you used to be a kind person back then and I meet you today as a mean person, I will merely infer the type of person you are as mean. Even though, someone else tells me how kind you were back then, I will not believe them because you were so mean to me and therefore a mean person according to my experience and view. So it really is about what and who you are now not then.

Consider some of the greatest musicians and actors as well. Joyous Celebration is still well-known because they're still doing great, not because they did well with their Joyous 5 album. You must move with the times, remain current and relevant and stop dwelling on what you did.

No CEO stays in that position because they made a very good decision and kept the company alive when it was at its lowest point 15 years ago. The CEO must continue making wise choices and ensuring more productivity and profit is made. The shareholders will not just say, 'oh its fine, she should stay CEO even when they're now slacking because once upon a time, she saved the company.' This is not how it works, no-one cares how good you used to be but everyone cares how good you are now.

CONTRARY TO POPULAR BELIEF, THE WORLD OWES YOU ABSOLUTELY NOTHING

A few years ago, my wife and I went to a funeral in the village she was born in, Mmakgabetlwane in the North West. At that time, we were driving this fancy car, you know how it goes when you go to your home-town, you rent a very nice car. Anyway, just after the funeral, my wife told me how one of her old-time friends said, "wuuu choma (my friend), please ask Siphiwe to give us tenders as well."

Besides the fact that she thought I look like a politician, what really upset me is how a woman over 30 can believe that someone from somewhere should give her a tender to change her life circumstances. It's almost as if people wait on life or others to move them to greener pastures. If you ever thought so and I really hope you don't because guess what, no-one will come to make your success happen, no-one is taking you anywhere and nobody's coming to your rescue!

Nobody owes you anything. The world doesn't owe you a thing. The company doesn't owe you the promotion you want and the market doesn't owe you a cent. You must be accountable. If you're going to get that promotion, it will be because you worked hard and did all that you had to do and more. It's all on you, it's all about what you do so don't blame anyone or any system for that matter. If you want someone to blame, simply look at the mirror. Blame yourself for what goes wrong and deal with your mistakes.

Contrary to what psychology says about the irrationality of an internal locus of control, that is, looking within yourself for all that goes wrong, it's actually much wiser to have an internal instead of external locus of control in this instance. Therefore, stop blaming the situation, the markets and global financial crisis for your broke state when you went out shopping to buy all the unnecessary things you knew you couldn't afford.

If things are bad in your life, don't look outside or beyond yourself to gather why they're going wrong. Before you start blaming anyone or pointing fingers, look at what you did wrong and how you can change it. If you feel disrespected, whether at work or within your network of friends, before you call people disrespectful, why don't you first look at the reasons why they think they can talk to you or treat you like that? Look at what's making you an object of disrespect first.

You can't be a clown at work and expect to get respect. Likewise, you can't be the friend that always says or does foolish things and expect your friends to take you serious. Unfortunately people treat us according to how we present ourselves and you show them what is permissible and what is not. So, if you feel mistreated or disrespected, look at how you gave them the reason first before you blame them for it.

Another issue is concerning genes. My goodness, the way we put so much blame on our family genes is sometimes unnecessarily exaggerated. I mean, if you're big like me, stop blaming the metabolism of your clan. Uh uh (seriously shaking head), shut up and go to gym, stop with the take outs and the see-food (seeing then eating) diet.

It's about time we become accountable and admit our wrongs and faults. No more blame-games and the 'it's them, not me' mentality. The sooner you acknowledge and confront the issues within you, the sooner you admit that you were wrong and at fault. The sooner you confront yourself and those issues, the quicker and better you can resolve and fix them. Stop giving blame where it's undue and start looking within because the world owes you absolutely nothing.

SMALL NOW, LARGE LATER....

One of the best investment strategies is to try and find a share that's small now but has potential to grow into the top companies in the JSE by Market Cap. This is the share that all the big investors are ignoring. In life, the sad reality is that you will be ignored when you're still small. Some movies have done a great portrayal of this by showing how that one quiet, nerdy, shy and chubby guy in school whom all the girls ignored grows up to be a successful and rich man and suddenly gets all the attention.

I'm sure you've seen and heard of similar stories in your neighbourhood or among your close circles. It's really unfortunate that people are taken seriously when they have 'improved' and are 'better' in looks, status, money and the likes. However, you should never despise small beginnings. You may be that guy right now or may have been. Whoever and wherever you are in life, just never underestimate small beginnings. You should in fact value them.

You may be small now but there's a great potential in you waiting to be explored and utilized. Very few people are born large, the rest and most of us are born small and I'm certain that most of you who are larger now can remember the days when you were still small. Give yourself the opportunity to grow and explore the potential in you. You don't have to be where you are today even in the next 10 years.

Most big people started small and out of nothing. They had no resources, wealth or the exposure they needed to get to where they are. Some only had a dream and others only a brain. The point is, you must take action to get further than where you are today. In itself, a dream is insufficient. In fact, a dream, vision and ambition without action are pretty much useless.

So take whatever minimal and small steps you need to. Do all that you have to do to get to where you need to be. Do not underestimate yourself even when others underestimate you. Take yourself seriously and believe in yourself and so will they. Set an example to others because people will treat you the way you treat yourself and allow them to.

In general, when the analysts criticize and limit your potential and capabilities, it's really bad enough that you have people perceiving you as an absolute waste of breath so the last thing you need is seeing yourself the way they do. Like I said before, don't live according to their marginal standards. Even when nobody's willing to bet a cent on you, bet a million on yourself.

Remember you're the greatest investment you can ever make so believe in yourself. Climb that ladder and stop complaining about where you are. Work to get to that larger place. Sometimes all you need is just your own self-belief, knowing and believing that you're going somewhere. Keep your drive, hope and ambition. You may be small now but you don't have to end there.

And when you eventually do get large, remember your journey and the days when you were still small.

Remember those that saw and gave you the chance and opportunity to explore your potential. Sometimes it's worth wondering where you might or might not have been if not for that one person.

If you know and see the potential in yourself then utilize it. Put it to work and believe that you won't always be where you are. It's always a process. Step by step you'll get there. Remember the baby steps: from sitting to crawling; from crawling to standing; from standing to walking; and from walking to running and the many more that follows. Take that potential and run with it. Take your first step today and move from the small place you're in to the larger arena.

BE PATIENT

"The stock market is designed to transfer money from the active to the patient." Warren Buffet

In the stock market, people are usually advised not to invest any amount of money if they would want it back within the period of one year or less. People are further advised to only invest a small percentage if they're going to need the money in a period of one to two years. The logic here is that the longer you wait the more money you can invest and therefore more money for your gain and less chances of a loss.

Therefore, one has to be patient during the years they have their money invested and be patient even through the storms that may hit the stock markets. It's very well-known that the stock markets are a risky, no guarantees investment and anything can happen. So how does an investor that has thousands and sometimes even millions of his money in the stock market, remain patient?

Well, it's pretty simple here, okay maybe not all that simple but it just has to appear so because there's unfortunately no other choice. This is because while the market is active and has a lot going on, both good and bad alike, the investor just has to be patient.

Sometimes this is the case with our life circumstances as well. We just have no other choice but to be patient no matter how hard it is. The reality of life is pretty much like the stock markets, sometimes there's really not much you can do besides to stay and wait. In such cases, no matter how much you want to get it done, no matter how much you may try to fix it, nothing can be done and all that you can do is wait.

The difficulty with patience can be seen as stemming from our need to be in control. We're so used to manipulating time, situations and a whole lot of other things that when we can't, we feel as though our sense of control has been lost. As a result, we tend to see everything as falling apart because things are just not going as planned or as they should be.

Well guess what, reality check… things will not always go according to plan. You'll make plans and they will fail. You'll be told that this will be done by tomorrow and it won't, you'll want things yet won't get them when and how you want them.

In such circumstances, that's when the only virtue you need to pursue is patience. You need to learn to be calm and relax when things don't go your way. You need to accept that okay, this is how things are, and I'm clearly not getting this thing when I really want it most. And yes, you'll be upset, angry and even have your day feeling messed up all because you can't be patient unless you choose to.

So the sooner you learn to be patient with yourself, others and situations, the better. Some people master this virtue more than others but wiser is he who possesses this valuable virtue. Patience is of much value because it helps you remain calm and free from the inevitable frustrations.

The difference between the patient and impatient person is that the former's waiting is more at ease than the latter. The latter's waiting is filled with anger and frustration and each day of waiting feels like hell. The former's waiting on the other hand, is characterised by understanding, acceptance and peace. They understand that sometimes things won't go as planned and just because something planned doesn't happen when it's supposed to happen does not necessarily mean it won't come to pass.

They accept that delays are inevitable in life and are wise enough to realise that it's better to remain at peace than be frustrated by things beyond their control. The patient person chooses to be realistic. This virtuous person sees and interprets things differently and that's why their waiting is better.

They don't see it as things getting out of control. They don't see emotions such as anger and frustration as necessary because they know it won't change a thing. Choose to be patient, choose to decide even before the frustrations set in that you won't be frustrated and when they do and you'll remain calm and be at peace in that situation even though it's frustrating.

Instead of complaining, grumbling and wasting your energy trying to get things done immediately when they can only be done tomorrow, rather accept that waiting is better than not waiting because trying to make it happen now will do nothing but exhaust you. The key problem with impatience is that it makes waiting uncomfortable and stressful so to avoid all this, rather make up your mind from the start. Sometimes it's better to accept things as they are and know that they'll work out eventually even though it's not in your preferred or expected time. So be patient my friend, it doesn't cost a cent and it's always for your own good.

THE JOB OF ANALYSTS IS TO TALK - THE JOB OF CHIEF EXECUTIVES IS TO RUN A BUSINESS

I've worked in a bank and I've seen how thorough executives prepare when there's an upcoming analyst presentation because analysts really interrogate executives. I happen to think that most analysts would like to be Chief Executives if they were given a chance but hey that's just a thought. In sports, for example, people become analysts mostly because they are too old to play, they were injured or simply because they love the sport but are not good enough to play.

If you're the CEO of your life then you better learn this now: leave the talking to the analysts and continue to run your business. Let whosoever who wants to talk do that but keep running your life. It's really sad to see people get discouraged, wrecked and even giving up because of what others say.

Analysts fit into different categories and serve multiple purposes. However, in any form of analysis required, there are common roles, qualities and characteristics regarded as significant. These include observation, paying attention to detail, critical thinking and pretty much playing the devil's advocate in some cases.

From the description I've just given, I'm sure you can now point out a few people you know and maybe even people in your life who fit this description so well they can be regarded as analysts. For the point I want to make here, we'll call them 'life analysts.' I doubt there's such a category in all analyst categories and perhaps I'm doing what clinical psychologists would identify as neologisms (new words formed by schizophrenic patients), but I promise you I'm not schizophrenic.

So these 'life analysts' are probably the first to see what's wrong with you, whatever you're doing or planning to do. They observe your life like hawks and look very closely only to identify errors. They usually have little positives and when they try, those are pretty much accompanied by a negative. I hope you now get what I mean.

The point is this, as the CEO of your life, you must know, understand and stay in your role. Your role includes managing, directing and deciding how to run your life so when the analysts and critics come your way, you must know and stand your ground. You should know what's right and do what you're supposed to be doing. I'm not saying you must disqualify every form of criticism you get because some are actually very constructive and helpful.

My point is only that you should never allow anyone to change the direction you see fit because they have something negative to say. Your job as CEO is to continue living and doing what's best for your company which in this case is your life. So when the critics talk, listen but listen with caution. Do not merely give up or stop doing what you're doing because they don't think it'll work.

In the end, it's your life, your choices and consequences to bear, so why let someone else decide what's best for you? Stop giving people control over your life when they don't have any. Some people don't even have 2% shares in your life yet they have an 80% say in what you do or don't do.

It's a great thing that we have friends, family, organisations and communities we can always turn to for advice. But bear the sad reality in mind that not everyone wants what's best for you. Some people don't want you to make it and some aren't very happy over your success and would love to see you fall. That's why it's very significant to choose whom you listen to.

Some people will hurt you and some will break you, some intentional and others not. Some people are there to build you up and others to pull you down. Some want the best and others just love it when you're at your worst. Some will bring out the best in you and still others will always bring out the worst in you. The fact is, whosoever plays any of these roles in your life does so because you allow them to.

You are not powerless, you are the CEO. You possess the power to determine what you will allow and refuse to permit in your life. You choose the effects that people and things have on you. Refuse to be helpless and release the power you possess. Don't allow anyone to push you away from your dreams and destiny, to make you think that your dreams are a mere fantasy or that you're way too ambitious. Don't allow yourself to live according to the standards set by the analysts.

Do not allow them to set your limits. Let them not tell you what you can or cannot do. In most cases all you really need to do is run your life like a CEO, and whether you're doing good or bad, they will talk because they always will. But just keep living. In all this, just keep calm and stay in control. Be in charge and stay in your role. The power of any company is always with the CEO. There's nothing they can do to you without your permission.

So live as one seated on the driver's seat because you have the steering wheel. Choose and stay in your direction. If it looks blurry to the analysts yet clear to you, keep driving. They will talk and grow weary, they will eventually get worn out and inevitably realise that their votes don't carry as much weight as yours. You have the final say, you have the final word. Run your life!

I hope you had an awesome read and grabbed some lessons for yourself. Remember to put what you've learned into practice…

BIBLIOGRAPHY

Busetti, F. 2009. The Effective Investor. South Africa: Rollerbird Press & Pan Macmillan SA.

Graham, B. & Zweig, J. 2003. The intelligent investor: revised edition. New York: HarperCollins Publishers.

Groz, M.M. 2009. Forbes Guide to the Markets. New York: John Wiley & Sons, Inc. (ISBN 978-0470463383)

Hagstrom, R.G. 2005. The Warren Buffet Way. 2nd edition.

Investopedia Staff. 2009. How Dividends Work for Investors. http://www.investopedia.com

Pilbeam, K. 2010. Finance and Financial Markets. Palgrave (ISBN 978-0230233218)

Profile's Stock Exchange Handbook 2013 – Issue 3 published by Profile Media Pty Ltd, July 2013

Seedat, Idris. 2013. Five for First-timers. The South African Financial Markets Journal. 18th edition.

Wright, R.E. & Quadrini, V. Money and Banking. "Chapter 2, Section 4: Financial Markets." Pp. 3 (1) Accessed June 20, 2012.

Quotes: www.brainyquote.com

Articles: www.saifm.co.za.

Pricing Power: www.wisegeek.com

Reports & Stats:

www.bdlive.co.za/national/2013/01/22/sa-more-unequal-than-20-years-ago-says-oxfam

www.oxfam.org/sites/www.oxfam.org/files/cost-of-inequality-oxfam-mb180113.pdf

www.leadershiponline.co.za/articles/finance/2080-economic-crisis

www.economist.com/node/21528581

www.economist.com/blogs/buttonwood/2012/07/economic

www.weforum.org/news/institutions-and-innovation-increasingly-important-competitiveness.

www.ingramcontent.com/pod-product-compliance
Lightning Source LLC
Chambersburg PA
CBHW051649170526
45167CB00001B/389